THE REALLY USEFUL
ULTIMATE
STUDENT
VEGETARIAN
COOK
BOOK

HELEN AITKEN

Published by Murdoch Books Pty Limited

Murdoch Books Australia
Pier 8/9, 23 Hickson Road, Millers Point NSW 2000
Phone: +61 (0) 2 8220 2000   Fax: +61 (0) 2 8220 2558

Murdoch Books UK Limited
Erico House, 6th Floor, 93-99 Upper Richmond Road
Putney, London SW15 2TG
Phone: +44 (0) 20 8785 5995   Fax: + 44 (0) 20 8785 5985

Chief Executive: Juliet Rogers
Concept: James Mills-Hicks
Design: Peta Nugent
Editor: Victoria Fisher
Production: Monique Layt
Printed in Hong Kong by Sing Cheong Printing Company Limited.

ISBN 978 1 74196 2475

RECIPE NOTES

 Degree of difficulty

 Approximate time required to prepare and cook each recipe.

 Indicates serving size

 Indicates dishes that are suitable for vegans

IMPORTANT: Those who might be at risk from the effects of salmonella poisoning (the elderly, pregnant women, young children and those suffering from immune deficiency diseases) should consult their doctor with any concerns about eating raw eggs.

CONVERSION GUIDE: You may find cooking times vary depending on the oven you are using. For fan-forced ovens, as a general rule, set the oven temperature to 20°C (70°F) lower than indicated in the recipe. We have used 20 ml (4 teaspoon) tablespoon measures. If you are using a 15 ml (3 teaspoon) tablespoon, for most recipes the difference will not be noticeable. However, for recipes using baking powder, gelatine, bicarbonate of soda, small amounts of flour and cornflour (cornstarch), add an extra teaspoon for each tablespoon specified.

CONTENTS

INTRODUCTION

A good vegetarian diet meets all today's requirements: it's nutritionally sound and both quick to prepare and easy to follow. With the days of overcooked vegetables and a-hundred-ways-with-soya-beans long gone, a vegetarian menu is now first choice for a growing number of students who care about their health and their finances.

A diet which overemphasises meat is a product of affluence (something not commonly found amongst today's cash-strapped students), and not necessarily a good one. Many people have recognised an imbalance in their way of eating and are modifying the amount of flesh foods they include in their diets. As people gain confidence, experiment more and discover the pleasures of cooking vegetarian foods they often welcome increased vitality and say goodbye to weight problems. Other potential benefits include clearer skin and less constipation. Many choose to abandon eating meat and fish altogether.

The term 'vegetarian' is used quite loosely. Some people call themselves vegetarian (or semi-vegetarian) while still eating a little fish or chicken and no red meat. Many just exclude all meat and fish from their diets. Vegans, on the other hand, exclude all other animal products such as milk, cheese and eggs as well. Most vegetarians, however, are lacto-ovo vegetarians who still eat eggs and dairy products. Meatless meals need never be bland or boring. They offer enormous variety, stimulating the imagination and sometimes offering the opportunity to learn new cooking skills. Vegetarian food, it could be argued, offers the student cook in particular, more scope to be inventive.

It is perfectly possible, and not at all difficult, for a busy student to lead a healthy life eating only vegetarian foods. The key is to ensure variety in the diet: eat as many different kinds of food as possible and all the essential nutrients that the body requires will be available.

It is important that any produce you buy be as fresh as possible so that the nutrients have not had time to deteriorate. For this reason, as well as for economy, it is a good idea to get into the habit of shopping and eating seasonally, when fruit and vegetables are at their best and cheapest.

Similarly, if at all possible, it is wise to freeze some fruits and vegetables when they are in season. Make sauces from tomatoes and red peppers (capsicums), purées from berries and stone fruits, and enjoy the taste of summer throughout the year.

You will be able to master many of these dishes even if you have never boiled an egg before! The recipes are straightforward and have been tested for success. They are the first steps to the healthy, balanced lifestyle that any successful student needs.
Happy cooking!

VEGANS

Vegans—those who eat only foods of plant origin and no animal products (dairy, eggs)—can obtain all their nutritional needs with just a little planning. Again, variety is the key. Vegans need to be especially vigilant about eating a variety of foods from the four plant food groups every day:

- grains in the form of bread, cereals, pasta and rice
- pulses, nuts and seeds including peanut butter and tahini, beans of all kinds (including baked beans), chickpeas, soy products (tofu, tempeh, soy milk—fortified with calcium and vitamin B12),
- vegetables
- fresh fruit and juices

Vegans need to make sure they do not miss out on Vitamin B12 as the usual sources in a lacto-ovo vegetarian diet are eggs and dairy products. Supplements may be necessary, although fortified soy milk is a good source. Mushrooms have plenty of vitamin B12, as does tofu. Soy milk also supplies calcium, as do some green vegetables, sesame seeds and tahini, almonds, and breads and cereals fortified with calcium. The iron which is found in meat and which lacto-ovo vegetarians can obtain from eggs can come also from pulses, soy products, green vegetables, breakfast cereals, dried fruits, nuts and seeds—provided you eat a wide variety. The amount of iron available from these foods is maximised if you eat them in conjunction with foods that are rich in vitamin C, such as oranges or blackcurrants. If you need something to keep you going late at night or between classes, snacks can include dried fruit, nuts, seeds and fresh fruit juice.

THE VEGETARIAN FOOD PYRAMID

It is as possible to have a poor diet eating exclusively vegetarian foods as it is eating excessive amounts of animal products. The Vegetarian Food Pyramid is a good starting point if you want to check whether your diet is adequate. Its principles are simple:

EAT MOST
- **grains:** barley, buckwheat, corn, rice, rye, millet, oats, wheat
- **foods made from grains:** bread, pasta, wholegrain breakfast cereals
- **fruit and vegetables**

EAT MODERATELY
- **dairy:** cheese, milk, yoghurt
- **pulses:** beans of all kinds, lentils, peas
- **nuts**
- **eggs**

EAT LEAST
- sugar, honey
- butter, cream
- margarine, oils
- alcohol, tea, coffee

Meal planning becomes easier if you make a habit of using the food pyramid as a guide.

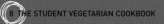

REALLY USEFUL VEGETARIAN TIPS

BONE UP ON CALCIUM

A significant percentage of people in the Western world don't consume enough calcium, leaving their bones at risk of osteo-porosis in old age. Nobody wants to be one of the statistics, so start taking active steps today to ensure your calcium levels are adequate. Unless you're vegan, it's likely that around 70% of the calcium in your daily diet comes from dairy foods, and adding a couple of extra serves of dairy a day is a simple way for most vegetarians to boost their calcium intake. For those whose diet doesn't include dairy foods, tofu can play a valuable role in maintaining calcium intake. Other important non-dairy sources of calcium are figs, sesame seeds and tahini, calcium-enriched soy milk, almonds, and some leafy green vegetables.

POWER-START YOUR MORNING

If you need energy to burn, muesli is an excellent way to start the day. Plus, the combination of dried fruit, bran, and pistachio nuts means that this dish is a very useful source of iron, which is also essential for energy.

WHY YOU NEED SEAWEED

Iodine is one of those nutrients that we only need in tiny quantities, but if you don't get enough, the results can be catastrophic. To keep up your iodine levels, add some seaweed to your diet. It's a simple solution, because you only need a small quantity to make a big difference — just adding a seaweed garnish to your soup or salad a few times a week should be adequate.

NUTS ADD MORE THAN CRUNCH TO YOUR SALAD

If you want to boost the nutritional power of your salad, just add some nuts. Walnuts provide a hard-to-find vegetarian source of the omega-3 fat alpha-linoleic acid, whilst pistachios offer a wide variety of vitamins and minerals. If you're after a protein boost, choose pine nuts which contain more protein by weight than any other nut or seed. And if you're concerned about your fat intake, get your nut fix from raw cashews as they are relatively low in fat.

STOCK UP ON SOY FOODS

Soy products such as tofu and tempeh — plus the beans themselves of course — should be a staple of every vegetarian kitchen. These are amongst the highest quality of any vegetarian protein source, and are versatile enough to be added to nearly any savoury dish. Tofu can be used in some sweet dishes too. Since it's a fermented food, tempeh is considered by some people to be a vegan source of vitamin B12, but unfortunately it isn't really — so if you're vegan, you'll still want to take a supplement.

WANT A LITTLE EXTRA?

Even the smallest changes to a dish can have a big effect on your nutritional intake. For example, just by sprinkling a few tablespoons of poppy seeds to baked vegetables, boosts the mineral content of a meal, adding extra calcium, iron, phosphorus, potassium, zinc and manganese. You can also achieve similar results by adding sunflower and sesame seeds to your brown rice, or almonds and ground linseeds to your porridge in the morning. Extra taste and extra nutrition!

BETA-CAROTENE MAKES UP FOR VITAMIN A SHORTFALLS

Make sure you include some orange-coloured fruit and vegetables, or dark green vegetables in your diet every day to provide you with the nutrient beta-carotene. Sometimes referred to as provitamin A, beta-carotene is a valuable antioxidant in its own right, but also has the benefit of being converted into vitamin A to meet the body's requirements. Since the oil-soluble form of vitamin A is predominantly found in animal foods, this is great news for vegetarians and vegans, who would otherwise be at risk of deficiency.

FOOD SAFETY

The most important thing to remember when you're responsible for feeding yourself, is to keep the kitchen clean. It isn't all that difficult to give yourself (or your house-mates) food poisoning, but if you cook your food carefully and observe basic hygiene and storage rules, you won't put anybody's health at risk. Here are a few pointers that you should keep in mind:

- Keep the kitchen floor clean, don't encourage mice, rats and other vermin to set up home in your house.

- Don't let dirty pots pile up or bacteria will multiply at an astonishing rate, making your kitchen unsafe and smelly. While you're cooking, try and wash-up as you go and finish off washing the rest straight after you've eaten.

- Wash up in very hot, soapy water. Use rubber gloves and a scrubbing brush and take care to rinse the dishes well with clean hot water.

- Leave the washing-up to air-dry on the draining board — dirty tea towels will just spread germs onto a clean plate, so make sure they're laundered regularly.

- Clean up splashes and spillages immediately after they occur as they make the floor dangerously slippery and can become ingrained and harbour bacteria. Bits of food on the floor and under the cooker can also encourage the odd mouse or two to set up home in your kitchen.

- Wash your hands before you start cooking.

- Keep the fridge clean. It's easy to forget a small lump of cheese that's left to go green at the back of the fridge, if it's not cleaned out regularly. Mould quickly spreads from bad food to healthy like the one bad apple in the sack. It's not only risky but costly.

- Never keep food past its use-by date.

- If a chilled item has been left out of the fridge and has become warm, play safe and throw it away, especially if it's made from dairy produce.

- If you are sharing facilities with someone who cooks meat make sure that they store raw meat properly wrapped up and well away from cooked foods. It is better to keep raw meat at the bottom of the fridge so that there's no danger of blood dripping down onto other food.

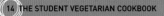

- Use a separate chopping board for raw meat as contamination (particularly from pork and poultry) to other foods is common. Scrub boards thoroughly after use.

- Wash your hands thoroughly after touching food.

- Store dry goods in a cool dark place. Keep bags sealed up with tape and check use-by dates.

- Take chilled or frozen food home as quickly as possible and store at the correct temperature. Don't refreeze food that has defrosted.

- Take care when defrosting food. Never force food to defrost quickly but leave it wrapped up at room temperature or even better, in the fridge until completely thawed. Don't ever be tempted by helpful friends who suggest 'rinsing the frozen prawns under the hot tap', or 'leaving the chicken in the sink full of hot water, or in the airing cupboard' to defrost.

- Don't reheat food more than once.

EQUIPMENT

Whether you choose to lodge in college accommodation or a shared house or flat, you'll probably have to share kitchen facilities with a group of other students. This can be a bit of a mixed bag of tricks. No doubt you will argue about whose turn it is to wash-up or empty the bin, but on the plus side, you will have the opportunity to pool resources, not just borrowing the ketchup from your house-mate's cupboard, but sharing kitchen utensils and equipment.

Every High Street has a cheap kitchen shop that's an Aladdin's Cave of useful gadgets from spatulas and can openers to salad spinners and fancy vegetable slicers, so you should be able to get your hands on the essentials listed below. And don't forget that any piece of equipment you buy, is an investment that you'll probably use for years.

A food processor or blender will repay your investment may times over so look in your local store for a keenly-priced brand.

ESSENTIALS

- can opener
- cheese grater
- rolling pin
- slotted spoon
- potato masher
- pastry brush

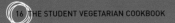

- chopping board
- 3 wooden spoons
- metal hand whisk
- metal sieve
- frying pan
- 3 sizes of saucepan with lids
- 2 sizes of bowl
- 1 large sharp knife and 1 small sharp knife
- blender or food processor if possible
- set of kitchen scales
- baking sheet (tray)
- casserole dish with lid
- vegetable peeler
- garlic press
- measuring jug
- wok

ESSENTIAL INGREDIENTS

If you only have half a cupboard and part of a shelf in a fridge or freezer to store your provisions, then you need to think carefully about what you buy or you will quickly run out of space. It is better to buy vegetables and salad ingredients as you require them but try and keep some of the following basics close to hand in order to make your meal preparation easier.

- packet of long grain rice
- can of chopped plum tomatoes
- can of baked beans
- small bottle of olive oil
- small bottle of high quality-vegetable oil
- bottle of soy sauce
- small bag of lentils
- small tub of dried parsley
- small tub of dried basil
- packet of vegetarian stock cubes
- tube of tomato purée
- bottle of vinegar

- small packet of flour

- bag of sugar

- salt and pepper

- jar of mustard of choice

- bottle of vegetarian Worcestershire sauce

- can of sweetcorn

- can of chickpeas

- cornflour

- bottle of tomato ketchup

- jar of honey

- jar of pesto sauce

- cumin seeds

- dried chillies

- carton of soy milk

- can of coconut milk/cream

- small tub of sour cream

- milk

- nonhydrogenated margarine

- eggs

SOUPS

INTRODUCTION

There's nothing quite like home-made soup, served piping hot with fresh bread. Making your own soup is enjoyable and surprisingly easy and the final dish can be dressed up or down to suit any occasion.

Many soups can be made in advance and do, in fact, benefit from overnight refrigeration as the flavours develop. Use commonsense to determine if any of the ingredients will not store well, for example if the soup has cream, add it when you are reheating for serving. The same goes for pasta; for instance, if you add the pasta to Minestrone, then leave it to sit around, it will be unpleasantly soggy. Generally soups can be kept for up to 3 days in the fridge, or frozen in airtight containers or freezer bags for 1–3 months. A lot of soups become very thick on standing and need to be diluted when reheated. Use more of the same stock, water or cream as appropriate. The seasoning will also need to be adjusted.

PUMPKIN SOUP

250 ml (9 fl oz/1 cup) vegetable stock

325 g (12 oz) butternut pumpkin (squash), cut into 1.5 cm ($^5/_8$ inch) cubes

1 onion, chopped

1 garlic clove, halved

$^1/_8$ teaspoon ground nutmeg

30 ml (1 fl oz/$^1/_8$ cup) cream (optional)

Choose pumpkins that are heavy for their size and have unblemished skins. Store whole at room temperature for up to one month. Wrap cut pumpkin in plastic wrap and store in the fridge.

Put the stock and 250 ml (9 fl oz/1 cup) water in a large heavy-based saucepan and bring to the boil.

Add the pumpkin, onion and garlic and return to the boil. Reduce the heat slightly and cook for 15 minutes, or until the pumpkin is soft.

Drain the vegetables through a colander, reserving the liquid. Purée the pumpkin mixture in a blender until smooth (you may need to add some of the reserved liquid). Return the pumpkin purée to the pan and stir in enough of the reserved liquid to reach the desired consistency. Season to taste with nutmeg, salt and cracked black pepper.

Ladle the soup into two soup bowls and pour some cream into each bowl to create a swirl pattern on the top. Serve with warm crusty bread.

REALLY EASY! · **40** MINUTES · SERVES **2** · VEGAN

CREAM OF FENNEL AND LEEK SOUP

Leeks often contain earth and dirt between their layers and need to be washed thoroughly. Trim the roots and remove any coarse outer leaves, then wash in a colander under running water. If using whole leeks, carefully separate out the leaves to rinse—making a cut halfway through to open the leaves. Wash the leek leaf end down so the dirt runs out.

Heat the butter in a large heavy-based saucepan, add the sliced fennel and leek, and cook, covered, over medium heat for 2–3 minutes, stirring occasionally.

Put the hot stock, rosemary sprigs and nutmeg in a saucepan and bring to the boil. Simmer over low heat for about 15 minutes, then remove the rosemary sprigs and add the fennel and leek mixture to the pan.

Transfer the soup to a blender or food processor and blend in batches until smooth. Return to the pan, and stir in the sour cream and parmesan. Reheat over medium heat until hot. Season to taste with salt and cracked black pepper and keep warm.

Spoon the soup into two warm soup bowls. Garnish with the extra parmesan and sour cream and serve immediately.

10 g ($^{1}/_{4}$ oz) butter

1 large fennel bulb, thinly sliced

1 leek, thinly sliced

400ml (14 fl oz/1$^{3}/_{4}$ cups) hot vegetable stock

1 rosemary sprig

pinch ground nutmeg

2 tablespoons sour cream

1 tablespoon finely grated parmesan cheese

grated parmesan cheese, extra, to garnish

sour cream, extra, to garnish

REALLY EASY! 35 MINUTES SERVES 2

POTATO AND SWEET CORN CHOWDER

2 cobs sweet corn

1 tablespoon vegetable oil

1/2 onion, finely diced

1 garlic clove , crushed

1/2 celery stalk, diced

1 small carrot,
peeled and diced

1 potato, peeled and diced

400 ml (14 fl oz/1 3/4 cups)
vegetable stock

1 tablespoon finely
chopped flat-leaf
(Italian) parsley

Don't buy or eat potatoes that have turned green. Cut out any eyes and sprouting, blackened or bruised areas from the potatoes before you use them. Store them in a brown paper bag in your food cupboard or some other cool, dark, dry place.

Bring a large pot of salted water to the boil, and cook the sweet corn for 5 minutes. Reserve 80 ml (2 1/2 fl oz/1/3 cup) of the cooking water. Cut the corn kernels from the cob, place half in a blender with the reserved cooking water, and blend until smooth.

Heat the oil in a large saucepan, add the onion, garlic, celery and a large pinch of salt and cook for 5 minutes. Add the carrot and potato, cook for a further 5 minutes, then add the stock, corn kernels and blended corn mixture. Reduce the heat and simmer for 20 minutes, or until the vegetables are tender. Season well, and stir in the chopped parsley before serving.

REALLY EASY! 50 MINUTES SERVES 2 VEGAN

MINESTRONE

Just about any vegetable can be added to minestrone, so this is a great recipe for using up odds and ends. Minestrone should always be accompanied by plenty of freshly grated parmesan—unless you are following a vegan diet of course!

Bring a saucepan of water to the boil, add the macaroni and cook for 10–12 minutes, or until tender. Drain.

Meanwhile, **heat** the oil in a large heavy-based saucepan, add the leek and garlic and cook over medium heat for 3–4 minutes.

Add the carrot, potato, courgettes, celery, green beans, tomato, stock and tomato paste. Bring to the boil, then reduce the heat and simmer for 10 minutes, or until the vegetables are tender.

Stir in the cooked pasta and cannellini beans and heat through. Spoon into warmed serving bowls and garnish with parsley and shaved parmesan.

REALLY EASY! · **40** MINUTES · SERVES **2** · VEGAN

40 g (1 $^1/_2$ fl oz/$^1/_4$ cup) macaroni

$^1/_2$ tablespoon olive oil

$^1/_2$ leek, sliced

1 garlic clove, crushed

$^1/_2$ carrot, sliced

$^1/_2$ waxy potato, chopped

$^1/_2$ courgette (zucchini), sliced

1 celery stalk, sliced

50 g (1$^3/_4$ oz) green beans, cut into short lengths

200 g (7 oz) tin chopped tomatoes

1 litre (35 fl oz/4 cups) vegetable stock

1 tablespoon tomato paste (purée)

200 g (7 oz) tin cannellini beans, rinsed and drained

1 tablespoon chopped flat-leaf (Italian) parsley

shaved Parmesan cheese, to serve (optional)

VEGETABLE SOUP

2 teaspoons olive oil

1/2 leek, halved lengthways and chopped

1/2 onion, diced

1 carrot, chopped

1 small celery stalk, chopped

$^1/_2$ courgette (zucchini), chopped

2 teaspoons tomato purée (paste)

400 ml (14 fl oz/2 cups) vegetable stock

150 g (5$^1/_2$ oz) butternut pumpkin (squash), cut into 2 cm ($^3/_4$ inch) cubes

1 potato, cut into 2 cm ($^3/_4$ inch) cubes

1 tablespoon chopped flat-leaf (Italian) parsley

215g (7$^1/_2$ oz) tin red kidney beans, or borlotti beans, drained and rinsed

This is an unbelievably easy, but tasty, soup that can happily be reheated the next day.

Heat the olive oil in a saucepan. Add the leek and onion and cook over medium heat for 2–3 minutes without browning, until they start to soften. Add the carrot, celery and courgette and cook for 3–4 minutes. Add the tomato paste and stir for 1 minute. Pour in the vegetable stock and 420 ml (14$^1/_2$ fl oz/1$^2/_3$ cups) water and bring to the boil. Reduce the heat to low and simmer for 20 minutes.

Add the pumpkin, potato, parsley and beans and simmer for a further 20 minutes, or until the vegetables are tender and the beans are cooked. Season well. Serve with crusty bread.

REALLY EASY! · **65** MINUTES · SERVES **2** · VEGAN

GAZPACHO

Gazpacho is a Spanish vegetable soup normally served chilled. It was originally made by field workers who pounded their bread and oil rations with water and salt and added whatever vegetables were available to the resulting soup. Gazpacho is Arabic in origin and means 'soaked bread'.

In a blender, **place** the tomatoes, cucumber, red pepper, onion, garlic, sourdough and 125 ml (4 fl oz/½ cup) cold water, and blend until smooth. Pass through a strainer into a bowl, and add the sherry vinegar. Season to taste with salt and Tabasco, then cover and refrigerate for at least 2 hours or overnight to allow the flavours to develop.

To make the dressing, **combine** all the ingredients in a small bowl. Season.

Stir the gazpacho well, then ladle into bowls. Spoon the dressing over the top before serving.

500g (1 lb 2 oz) vine-ripened tomatoes, chopped

½ Lebanese (short) cucumber, chopped

½ red pepper (capsicum), seeded and chopped

½ red onion, chopped

1 garlic clove

40 g (1½ oz) sourdough bread, crusts removed

1 tablespoon sherry vinegar

Tabasco sauce

Dressing

1 teaspoon each of finely diced tomato, red pepper (capsicum), red onion, Lebanese (short) cucumber

1 teaspoon finely chopped flat-leaf (Italian) parsley

½ tablespoon extra virgin olive oil

½ teaspoon lemon juice

LAKSA

100 g (3^1/$_2$ oz) dried
rice vermicelli

1 tablespoon peanut oil

1–2 tablespoons
laksa paste

500 ml (17 fl oz/2 cups)
vegetable stock

375 ml (13 fl oz/1^1/$_2$ cups)
coconut milk

125 g (4^1/$_2$ oz) snowpeas
(mangetout), halved
diagonally

2 spring onions
(scallions), cut into 3 cm
(1^1/$_4$ inch) lengths

1 tablespoon lime juice

60 g (2^1/$_4$ oz) bean sprouts

100g (3^1/$_2$ oz) fried tofu
puffs, halved

1^1/$_2$ tablespoons roughly
chopped Vietnamese mint

1 large handful coriander
(cilantro) leaves

Many brands of laksa paste contain shrimp paste or fish sauce so make sure you buy a suitable vegetarian brand for this tasty recipe.

Place the vermicelli in a large bowl, cover with boiling water and soak for 5 minutes.

Heat the oil in a large saucepan, add the laksa paste and cook, stirring, over medium heat for 1 minute, or until fragrant. Add the stock, coconut milk, snowpeas and spring onion and simmer for 5 minutes. Pour in the lime juice and season to taste with salt and freshly ground black pepper.

Drain the vermicelli and divide among two bowls. Top with the bean sprouts and fried tofu puffs. Ladle the hot soup into the bowls and sprinkle with the fresh mint and coriander. Serve immediately.

REALLY EASY! · 25 MINUTES · SERVES 2

FRESH MUSHROOM, SHALLOT AND
SOUR CREAM SOUP

For an ideal garnish to this tasty soup, fry diced button mushrooms in a little butter until golden. This can be prepared during the soup's final simmering and will impress your friends greatly!

Melt the butter in a large heavy-based saucepan and add the shallots, garlic and parsley. Cook over medium heat for 2–3 minutes. Put the stock and milk in a separate saucepan and bring to the boil.

Gently wipe the mushrooms, then chop and add to the shallot mixture. Season with salt and pepper, and stir in the nutmeg and cayenne pepper. Cook, stirring, for 1 minute. Add the stock and milk, bring to the boil, then reduce the heat and simmer for 5 minutes. Transfer the soup to a blender or food processor and blend until smooth. Return to the pan.

Stir in the sour cream, adjust the seasoning and reheat gently. Serve sprinkled with cayenne pepper.

REALLY EASY! 25 MINUTES SERVES 2

1 tablespoon butter

50 g (about 2) French shallots, roughly chopped

1 garlic clove, crushed

1 large handful flat-leaf (Italian) parsley

160 ml ($5^{1}/_{4}$ fl oz/$^{3}/_{4}$ cup) vegetable stock

160 ml ($5^{1}/_{4}$ fl oz/$^{3}/_{4}$ cup) milk

300 g ($10^{1}/_{2}$ oz) button mushrooms

pinch ground nutmeg

pinch cayenne pepper

75 g ($2^{1}/_{2}$ oz) light sour cream

cayenne pepper, to garnish

CARROT AND GINGER SOUP

375 ml (13 fl oz/1 1/2 cups) vegetable stock

1/2 tablespoon oil

1/2 onion, chopped

1/2 tablespoon grated fresh ginger

500g (1 lb 2oz) carrots, chopped

1 tablespoon chopped coriander (cilantro) leaves

This delicious soup can be served with crusty bread for a warming winter supper. Make double the quantity and reheat the next day.

Place the stock in a pan and bring to the boil. Heat the oil in a large heavy-based pan, add the onion and ginger and cook for 2 minutes, or until the onion has softened.

Add the stock and carrots. Bring to the boil, then reduce the heat and simmer for 10–15 minutes, or until the carrot is cooked and tender.

Place in a blender or food processor and process in batches until smooth. Return to the pan and add a little more stock or water to thin the soup to your preferred consistency.

Stir in the coriander and season to taste. Heat gently before serving.

REALLY EASY! · 30 MINUTES · SERVES 2 · VEGAN

ASPARAGUS SOUP

375 g (13 oz) fresh
asparagus spears

500 ml (18 fl oz/2 cup)
vegetable stock

15 g (1/2 oz) butter

1/2 tablespoon plain
(all-purpose) flour

1/2 teaspoon finely
grated lemon zest

extra lemon zest,
to garnish

Asparagus is widey available and can make a tasty change from other vegetables. It doesn't keep for long and should really be cooked on the day of purchase. Store in the fridge wrapped in plastic for 3-4 days, or stand the bundle in a container of water and cover with a plastic bag. To prepare, snap off the woody bottom of the asparagus spear and peel away any woody stems.

Trim and discard any woody ends from the asparagus spears and cut into 2 cm (3/4 inch) lengths. Place in a large saucepan and add 250 ml (9 fl oz/1 cup) of the stock. Cover and bring to the boil, then cook for 10 minutes, or until the asparagus is tender.

Transfer the asparagus and the hot stock to a blender or food processor, and purée in batches until smooth. Melt the butter in the saucepan over low heat, add the flour, then cook, stirring, for about 1 minute, or until pale and foaming. Remove from the heat and gradually add the remaining stock, stirring until smooth after each addition. When all the stock has been added, return the saucepan to the heat, bring to the boil, then simmer for 2 minutes.

Add the asparagus purée to the pan and stir until combined. When heated through, stir in the lemon zest and season with salt and cracked black pepper. Garnish with the lemon zest.

REALLY EASY!

30 MINUTES

SERVES **2**

SWEET POTATO AND CHILLI SOUP

Sweet potatoes are not true potatoes at all but they taste delicious in this spicy soup. Remember that sweet potatoes don't keep for as long as potatoes and will only last for more than a few days if kept in a cool, dry place. Be sure not to rub your eyes when preparing the chillies!

Heat the oil in a large heavy-based saucepan, add the onion and cook for 1–2 minutes, or until soft. Add the garlic, chilli and paprika and cook for a further 2 minutes, or until aromatic. Add the sweet potato to the pan and toss to coat with the spices.

Pour in the stock, bring to the boil, then reduce the heat and simmer for 15 minutes, or until the vegetables are tender. Cool slightly, then transfer to a blender or food processor and blend in batches until smooth, adding extra water if needed to reach the desired consistency. Do not overblend or the mixture may become gluey.

Season to taste with salt and black pepper. Ladle the soup into bowls, sprinkle with dried chilli and serve.

$^1/_2$ tablespoon oil

$^1/_2$ onion, chopped

1 garlic clove , finely chopped

1 small red chilli, finely chopped

pinch paprika

375 g (13 oz) orange sweet potato, chopped into small pieces

500 ml (17 fl oz/2 cups) vegetable stock

chopped dried chilli, to garnish

REALLY EASY! **35** MINUTES SERVES **2** VEGAN

SPLIT PEA AND VEGETABLE SOUP

½ tablespoon peanut
or vegetable oil

½ onion, chopped

1 garlic clove, chopped

1 teaspoon chopped
fresh ginger

¾ tablespoon Madras
curry paste

50 g (1¾ oz) yellow split
peas, rinsed and drained

½ large courgette
(zucchini), peeled
and chopped

½ large carrot,
roughly chopped

85 g (3 oz) button
mushrooms,
roughly chopped

½ celery stalk,
roughly chopped

500 ml (17 fl oz/2 cups)
vegetable stock

60 ml (2 fl oz/¼ cup)
cream

Split peas are an important protein source and this tasty soup is a simple way of keeping your daily intake on target.

Heat the oil in a saucepan, add the onion and cook over low heat for 5 minutes, or until soft. Add the garlic, ginger and curry paste and cook over medium heat for 2 minutes. Stir in the split peas until well coated with paste, then add the courgette, carrot, mushroom and celery and cook for 2 minutes.

Add the stock, bring to the boil, then reduce the heat and simmer, partly covered, for 1 hour. Remove from the heat and allow to cool slightly.

Transfer the soup to a blender or food processor and process in batches until smooth. Return to the pan, stir in the cream and gently heat until warmed through. Delicious served with naan bread.

REALLY EASY! — 1½ HOURS — SERVES 2

PEPPER, SPINACH AND CHICKPEA SOUP

Serve this hearty soup with thick slices of buttered toast for a filling and economical meal.

Heat the oil in a large heavy-based saucepan and stir in the spring onion. Reduce the heat and cook, covered, for 2–3 minutes, or until softened. Meanwhile, remove the seeds and membrane from the pepper and finely dice. Add the pepper, garlic and cumin seeds to the pan and cook for 1 minute.

Add the passata and stock and bring the mixture to the boil. Reduce the heat and simmer for 10 minutes. Add the chickpeas, vinegar and sugar to the soup and simmer for a further 5 minutes.

Stir in the baby spinach and season to taste with salt and ground black pepper. Cook until the spinach begins to wilt, then serve immediately.

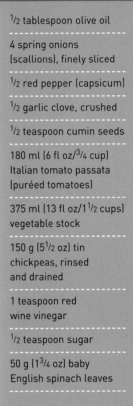

1/2 tablespoon olive oil

4 spring onions (scallions), finely sliced

1/2 red pepper (capsicum)

1/2 garlic clove, crushed

1/2 teaspoon cumin seeds

180 ml (6 fl oz/3/4 cup) Italian tomato passata (puréed tomatoes)

375 ml (13 fl oz/1 1/2 cups) vegetable stock

150 g (5 1/2 oz) tin chickpeas, rinsed and drained

1 teaspoon red wine vinegar

1/2 teaspoon sugar

50 g (1 3/4 oz) baby English spinach leaves

BORSCHT (COLD BEETROOT SOUP)

2 large (500g/1 lb 2 oz) beetroot, peeled

----

2 teaspoons caster (superfine) sugar

----

2 tablespoons lemon juice

----

1 egg

----

sour cream, to serve (optional)

If you want to make this soup extra tasty add a dash of sour cream before you serve it.

Grate the beetroot, and place in a saucepan with the caster sugar and 750 ml (26 fl oz/3 cups) water. Stir over low heat until the sugar has dissolved. Simmer, partially covered, for about 30 minutes, skimming the surface occasionally.

Add the lemon juice and simmer, uncovered, for 10 minutes. Remove the pan from the heat.

Whisk the egg in a bowl. Gradually pour the egg into the beetroot mixture, whisking constantly and taking care not to curdle the egg. Season to taste with salt and pepper. Allow the soup to cool, then cover and refrigerate until cold. Delicious served with a dollop of sour cream.

EASY! · 45 MINUTES · SERVES 2

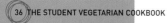

GREEN CURRY VEGETABLE SOUP

This is another of those recipes which will quickly become a favourite. The lime leaf and limes do add to the cost of this dish but they really enhance the flavour and if you make large quantities that extra cost will be small. Limes are green because they are picked before they ripen so they will keep for some time.

Heat the oil in a large saucepan and add the curry paste and lime leaves. Cook, stirring, over medium heat for 1 minute, or until the mixture is fragrant. Bring the stock to the boil in a separate saucepan.

Gradually **add** the stock and coconut milk to the curry mixture and bring to the boil. Add the pumpkin, squash and corn, and simmer over low heat for 12 minutes, or until the pumpkin is tender.

Add the soy sauce and lime juice, and season to taste with sugar, salt and black pepper. Sprinkle with the mint before serving.

REALLY EASY! 35 MINUTES SERVES 2

1 teaspoon peanut oil

1–2 teaspoons green curry paste

1 makrut (kaffir lime) leaf

400ml (14 fl oz) vegetable stock

250 ml (9 fl oz/1cup) coconut milk

200 g (7 oz) butternut pumpkin (squash), cut into 1.5 cm (^{5}/8 inch) cubes

85 g (3 oz) small yellow squash (pattypan squash), sliced

40 g (1^1/2 oz) fresh baby corn spears, halved lengthways

3 teaspoons mushroom soy sauce

3 teaspoons lime juice

^{1}/2 teaspoon sugar

2 teaspoons Vietnamese mint, finely chopped

SPINACH SOUP

15 g (1/2 oz) butter

1/2 onion, finely chopped

250 g (9 oz) floury potatoes, grated

500 ml (17 fl oz/2 cups) vegetable stock

250 g (9 oz) frozen chopped English spinach

pinch ground nutmeg

sour cream, to serve

This is one of those dishes that you can double the quantities and reheat the following day. If you can't get hold of fresh spinach, use frozen leaf spinach instead. and a healthier alternative to the sour cream would be natural yoghurt.

Melt the butter in a large saucepan, add the chopped onion and cook, stirring occasionally, until soft but not browned.

Add the potato and stock to the pan and mix well, scraping the onion from the bottom of the pan. Add the unthawed blocks of spinach and cook, covered, until the spinach has thawed and broken up, stirring occasionally. Uncover and simmer for 10–15 minutes, or until the potato is very soft. Stir the soup frequently while it cooks to prevent it sticking on the bottom. Transfer to a blender or food processor and blend in batches until smooth.

Return the soup to the pan and gently reheat. Add the nutmeg, and season with salt and black pepper. Ladle into bowls, add a dollop of sour cream to each bowl and swirl into the soup.

REALLY EASY! · 35 MINUTES · SERVES 2

PUMPKIN AND RED LENTIL SOUP

Tahini is a thick oily paste extracted from husked white sesame seeds, The name comes from the Arab word *tahana*, meaning to grind or crush. Tahini paste is available as both dark and light paste–the latter of which is usually of the better quality. Always take care when transfering hot soups to the blender.

Heat the oil in a large saucepan over medium heat, add the chilli and onion and cook for 2–3 minutes, or until the onion is soft. Reduce the heat to low, add the pumpkin and sweet potato and cook, covered, for 8 minutes, stirring occasionally.

Increase the heat to high, add the stock and bring to the boil. Reduce the heat to low, and simmer, covered, for 10 minutes. Add the red lentils and cook, covered, for 7 minutes, or until tender.

Process the soup in batches in a blender or food processor, add the tahini and blend until smooth. Return to the saucepan and gently heat until warmed through. Garnish with chilli.

$^1/_2$ tablespoon olive oil

$^1/_2$ long red chilli, seeded and chopped

$^1/_2$ onion, finely chopped

250 g (9 oz) butternut pumpkin (squash), chopped

175 g (6 oz) orange sweet potato, chopped

750 ml (26 fl oz/3 cups) vegetable stock

60 g (2$^1/_4$ fl oz/$^1/_4$ cup) red lentils

$^1/_2$ tablespoon tahini

red chilli, extra, to garnish

EASY! 45 MINUTES SERVES 2 VEGAN

SPICY PARSNIP SOUP

400 ml (14 fl oz/1^3/$_4$ cups) vegetable stock

10 g (^{1}/$_4$ oz) butter

^{1}/$_2$ white onion, cut into quarters and finely sliced

^{1}/$_2$ small leek, finely sliced

175 g (6 oz) parsnips, peeled and finely sliced

1–2 teaspoons Madras curry powder

^{1}/$_4$ teaspoon ground cumin

100 ml (3^1/$_2$ fl oz/^{1}/$_2$ cup) cream

1^1/$_2$ teaspoons coriander (cilantro) leaves

When buying parsnips choose firm, smooth vegetables. Particularly large or old parsnips may need their core removed before cooking as they can be hard, flavourless and very fibrous. Parsnips will keep in the fridge for four weeks. If your student budget is under pressure then this soup is equally delicious without the cream.

Bring the stock to the boil in a saucepan and keep at a low simmer.

Place the butter in a large saucepan and melt over medium heat. Add the onion, leek and parsnip and cook, covered, for 5 minutes. Add the curry powder and cumin and cook for 1 minute. Stir in the stock and cook, covered, over medium heat for about 10 minutes, or until tender.

Transfer the soup to a blender or food processor and blend in batches until smooth. Return to the pan. Stir in the cream and warm through over low heat. Season to taste with salt and cracked black pepper and scatter with coriander leaves.

REALLY EASY! · 35 MINUTES · SERVES 2

CHICKPEA, POTATO AND SPINACH SOUP

This rich soup is so simple to make but tastes truly exotic. Why not serve it to friends after an evening at the cinema or on the sports field?

Place the stock in a saucepan, then cover and slowly bring to the boil. Heat the olive oil in a large heavy-based saucepan, and cook the onion for 2–3 minutes, or until soft.

Add the potato to the onion, and stir in the paprika, garlic and chickpeas. Add the onion mixture to the stock and bring to the boil. Stir in the tomato, and season with salt and cracked black pepper.

Simmer for 10 minutes, or until the potato is tender. Add the spinach and cook until wilted. Top with parmesan, season to taste and serve.

REALLY EASY! · 35 MINUTES · SERVES 2 · VEGAN

500 ml (18 fl oz/2 cups) vegetable stock

³/₄ tablespoon olive oil

¹/₂ onion, finely chopped

¹/₂ large potato, cut into 1.5 cm (⁵/₈ inch) cubes

³/₄ teaspoon paprika

1 garlic clove, crushed

200 g (7 oz) tin chickpeas, drained

¹/₂ large tomato, cut into small cubes

25 g (1 oz/¹/₂ cup) English spinach, coarsely shredded

15 g (¹/₂ oz) grated parmesan cheese (optional)

GREEN SOUP WITH PISTOU

2 tablespoons olive oil

1/2 onion, finely chopped

1 garlic clove, crushed

1/2 celery stalk, chopped

1/2 courgette (zucchini), cut into 1 cm (1/2 inch) rounds

1/2 head broccoli, cut into 1 cm (1/2 inch) pieces

750 ml (26 fl oz/3 cups) vegetable stock

75 g (2 3/4 oz) green beans, trimmed and cut into 1 cm (1/2 inch) pieces

80 g (2 3/4 oz/1/2 cup) green peas

80 g (1/2 bunch) asparagus, ends trimmed and cut into 1 cm (1/2 inch) pieces

40 g (1 1/2 oz/1 cup) shredded silverbeet (Swiss chard) leaves

Pistou

1 garlic clove, peeled

2 small handfuls basil

40 ml (1 1/4 fl oz) olive oil

25 g (1 oz/1/4 cup) grated parmesan cheese

Don't be put off by the list of ingredients and that strange word pistou! This is one of those dishes which will repay your efforts ten times over! If you are looking to impress some college friends then this dish should certainly be on the menu!

Heat the olive oil in a large saucepan, and cook the onion, garlic and celery until golden. Add the courgette and broccoli, and cook for 5 minutes.

Add the stock and bring to the boil. Simmer for 5 minutes, then add the green beans, peas, asparagus and silverbeet. Simmer for 5 minutes, or until the vegetables are tender. Season well with salt and pepper.

To make the pistou, **place** the garlic and basil in a mortar and pestle or small food processor and crush together. Slowly add the oil, and blend until a smooth paste. Stir in the parmesan, and season well with salt and pepper.

Ladle the soup into bowls and serve with a dollop of pistou.

EASY! · 45 MINUTES · SERVES 2

CURRIED LENTIL, CARROT AND
CASHEW SOUP

If you feel like giving this tasty soup an extra kick then garnish with a pinch of chilli flakes.

Bring the stock to the boil in a large saucepan. Add the carrots and lentils, bring the mixture back to the boil, then simmer over low heat for about 8 minutes, or until the carrot and lentils are soft.

Meanwhile, **heat** the oil in a pan, add the onion and cashews and cook over medium heat for 2–3 minutes, or until the onion is soft and browned. Add the curry paste and coriander and cook for a further 1 minute, or until fragrant. Stir the paste into the carrot and lentil mixture.

Transfer to a food processor or blender and process in batches until smooth. Return the mixture to the pan and reheat over medium heat until hot. Season to taste with salt and cracked black pepper and serve with a dollop of yoghurt and a sprinkling of coriander.

REALLY EASY!   **25 MINUTES**   **SERVES 2**

500 ml (52 fl oz/2 cups) vegetable stock

- - - - - - - - - - - - - - - - - - - -

250 g (9 oz) carrots, grated

- - - - - - - - - - - - - - - - - - - -

60 g (2^{1}/$_4$ oz/^{1}/$_4$ cup) red lentils, rinsed and drained

- - - - - - - - - - - - - - - - - - - -

^{1}/$_2$ tablespoon olive oil

- - - - - - - - - - - - - - - - - - - -

^{1}/$_2$ large onion, chopped

- - - - - - - - - - - - - - - - - - - -

40 g (1^{1}/$_2$ oz/^{1}/$_4$ cup) unsalted cashew nuts

- - - - - - - - - - - - - - - - - - - -

^{1}/$_2$ tablespoon Madras curry paste

- - - - - - - - - - - - - - - - - - - -

1 large handful chopped coriander (cilantro) leaves and stems

- - - - - - - - - - - - - - - - - - - -

60 g (2^{1}/$_4$ oz/ ^{1}/$_4$ cup) Greek-style yoghurt

- - - - - - - - - - - - - - - - - - - -

coriander (cilantro) leaves, to garnish

- - - - - - - - - - - - - - - - - - - -

SOBA NOODLE AND VEGETABLE SOUP

125 g (4¹/₂ oz)
soba noodles

1 dried shiitake mushroom

1 litre (35 fl oz/4 cups)
vegetable stock

60 g (2¹/₄ oz) snowpeas
(mangetout), cut into strips

1 small carrot, cut into
thin 5 cm (2 inch) strips

1 garlic clove,
finely chopped

3 spring onions
(scallions), cut into 5 cm
(2 inch) lengths and
thinly sliced lengthways

1.5 cm (²/₃ inch)
piece ginger, cut into
julienne strips

40 ml (1¹/₄ fl oz) soy sauce

30 ml (1 fl oz) mirin
or sake

45 g (¹/₂ cup) bean sprouts

coriander (cilantro)
leaves, to garnish

This is another of those recipes which may look daunting to a student cook but is in fact really simple. If you make more than one quantity and shop for the vegetables at a local supermarket on the day that you intend to make the dish, you will have an incredibly economical and tasty soup that you will want to eat again and again.

Cook the noodles according to the packet instructions. Drain.

Soak the mushroom in 125 ml (4 fl oz/¹/₂ cup) boiling water until soft. Drain, reserving the liquid. Remove the stalk and slice the mushroom.

Combine the stock, mushrooms, reserved liquid, snowpeas, carrot, garlic, spring onion and ginger in a large saucepan. Bring slowly to the boil, then reduce the heat to low and simmer for 5 minutes, or until the vegetables are tender. Add the soy sauce, mirin and bean sprouts. Cook for a further 3 minutes.

Divide the noodles among two large serving bowls. Ladle the hot liquid and vegetables over the top and garnish with coriander.

REALLY EASY! — 35 MINUTES — SERVES 2 — VEGAN

ZUPPA DI FAGIOLI

This recipe is the authentic bean soup from Florence. If you like, spice it up by adding chopped chilli.

Put half a tin of beans and liquid in a blender or small food processor and blend until smooth. Drain the other half, reserving the beans and discarding the liquid.

Heat the oil in a large heavy-based saucepan, add the leek, garlic and thyme and cook for 2–3 minutes, or until soft and aromatic. Add the celery, carrot, silverbeet and tomato and cook for a further 2–3 minutes, or until the silverbeet has wilted. Heat the stock in a separate saucepan.

Stir the puréed cannellini beans and stock into the vegetable mixture. Bring to the boil, then reduce the heat and simmer for 5–10 minutes, or until the vegetables are tender. Add the drained beans and stir until heated through. Season to taste with salt and cracked black pepper.

Arrange 2 slices of roll in the base of each soup bowl. Stir the balsamic vinegar into the soup and ladle over the bread. Serve topped with grated parmesan.

1 x 400 g (14 oz) tin cannellini beans

$1/2$ tablespoon extra virgin olive oil

$1/2$ leek, finely chopped

1 garlic clove, crushed

1 teaspoon thyme leaves

1 celery stalk, diced

$1/2$ carrot, diced

500 ml (17 fl oz/1 lb 2 oz) silverbeet (Swiss chard), trimmed and roughly chopped

$1/2$ ripe tomato, diced

500 ml (2 cups) vegetable stock

1 small crusty roll, cut into 4 slices

1 teaspoon balsamic vinegar

15 g ($1/2$ oz) finely grated parmesan cheese (optional)

REALLY EASY! 30 MINUTES SERVES 2 VEGAN

COLD SPICY ROAST PEPPER SOUP

2 red peppers (capsicums)

1 teaspoon oil

1 garlic clove, crushed

2 spring onions (scallions), sliced

$^1/_2$ teaspoon finely chopped seeded chillies

210 g (7$^1/_2$ oz) tin chopped tomatoes

60 ml (2 fl oz/$^1/_4$ cup) chilled vegetable stock

$^1/_2$ teaspoon balsamic vinegar

1 tablespoon chopped basil

This is a wonderful soup that you can keep in the fridge for those days when you are running late or just too stressed after a class to cook something fresh. A great standby for any student kitchen.

Cut the peppers into quarters and remove the seeds and membrane. Place the peppers skin-side up under a hot grill (broiler) and grill until the skins blacken and blister. Cool in a plastic bag, then peel away the skin and roughly chop the flesh.

Heat the oil in a small saucepan, add the garlic, spring onion and chilli, and cook over low heat for 1–2 minutes, or until softened.

Transfer to a food processor or blender, and add the pepper, chopped tomatoes and stock. Blend until smooth, then stir in the vinegar and basil. Season to taste with salt and cracked pepper. Refrigerate, then serve cold.

REALLY EASY! · 25 MINUTES · SERVES 2 · VEGAN

SILVERBEET AND RISONI SOUP WITH
GRUYÈRE CROUTONS

OK, this soup takes a little longer to prepare than the others but as most of that time is for simmering you aren't tied to the cooker. Catch up with some emails or simple revision, just make sure that you check back occasionally to ensure the pot hasn't boiled dry or is about to explode!

Heat the butter in a large heavy-based saucepan, add the onion and garlic and cook over medium heat for 2–3 minutes, or until the onion is softened. Meanwhile, place the stock in a separate pan and bring to the boil.

Add the stock to the onion mixture and bring to the boil. Add the risoni, reduce the heat and simmer for 8 minutes, stirring occasionally.

Meanwhile, **place** the baguette slices in a single layer on a baking tray and cook under a preheated grill (broiler) until golden brown on one side. Turn the slices over and brush with the combined melted butter and mustard. Top with the Gruyère and grill until the cheese has melted.

Add the silverbeet and basil to the risoni mixture and simmer for about 1 minute, or until the risoni is *al dente* and the silverbeet is cooked. Season with salt and freshly ground black pepper and serve with the gruyère croutons.

10 g (1/4 oz) butter

1/2 onion, finely chopped

1 garlic clove, crushed

670 ml (23 fl oz/2²/3 cups) vegetable stock

65 g (2¹/2 oz/¹/3 cup) risoni

1/4 baguette, cut into 6 slices

5 g (1/8 oz) butter, extra, melted

1/2 teaspoon dijon mustard

15 g (1/2 oz) gruyère cheese, coarsely grated

165 g (5³/4 oz) silverbeet (Swiss chard), central stalk removed, shredded

4 tablespoons basil, torn

EASY! **30** MINUTES SERVES **2**

CHILLI, CORN AND RED PEPPER SOUP

1/2 coriander (cilantro) sprig

2 cobs sweet corn

15 g (1/2 oz) butter

1 red pepper (capsicum), diced

1/2 small onion, finely chopped

1/2 small red chilli, finely chopped

1/2 tablespoon plain (all-purpose) flour

250 ml (9 fl oz/1 cup) vegetable stock

60 ml (2 fl oz/1/4 cup) cream

I love to serve this stunning soup with with grilled cheese on pitta bread. It's the perfect pick-me-up after a hard day at college.

Trim the leaves off the coriander and finely chop the root and stems. Cut the kernels off the corn cobs.

Heat the butter in a saucepan over medium heat. Add the corn kernels, pepper, onion and chilli and stir to coat in the butter. Cook, covered, over low heat, stirring occasionally, for 10 minutes, or until soft. Increase the heat to medium, add the coriander root and stem and cook, stirring, for 30 seconds, or until fragrant. Sprinkle with the flour and stir for 1 minute. Remove from the heat and gradually stir in the stock. Add 250 ml (9 fl oz/ 1 cup) water and return to the heat. Bring to the boil, reduce the heat to low and simmer, covered, for 30 minutes, or until the vegetables are tender. Cool slightly.

Ladle 250 ml (9 fl oz/1 cup) of the soup into a blender and purée until smooth. Return the purée to the soup in the pan, pour in the cream and gently heat until warmed through. Season. Sprinkle with the coriander leaves and serve. Delicious with grilled cheese on pitta bread.

REALLY EASY! · 1 HOUR · SERVES 2

THAI SPICY SOUR SOUP

This is a delightful dish but for true vegetarian cooking, make sure you buy a brand of Tom Yum paste that does not contain shrimp paste or fish sauce. Tom Yum paste is available at all Asian supermarkets and is a hot sauce which normally includes ingredients such as lemongrass, lime leaves, onions, mint, tamarind, coriander and basil.

Place the stock, Tom Yum paste, galangal, lemongrass, kaffir lime leaves, chilli and 375 ml (13 fl oz/1^{1}/2 cups) water in a saucepan. Cover and bring to the boil, then reduce the heat and simmer for 5 minutes.

Add the mushrooms and tofu and simmer for 5 minutes, or until the mushrooms are tender. Add the bok choy and simmer for a further minute, or until wilted. Remove the pan from the heat and stir in the lime juice and coriander leaves before serving.

REALLY EASY! | 30 MINUTES | SERVES 2

375 ml (13 fl oz/1^{1}/2 cups) vegetable stock

1 tablespoon Tom Yum paste

1 cm x 1 cm (^{1}/2 inch x ^{1}/2 inch) piece galangal, peeled and cut into thin slices

^{1}/2 stem lemongrass, lightly crushed and cut into 4 lengths

1 fresh makrut (kaffir lime) leaf

^{1}/2 small red chilli, finely sliced on the diagonal (optional)

100 g (3^{1}/2 oz) button mushrooms, halved

100 g (3^{1}/2 oz) silken firm tofu, cut into 1.5 cm (^{5}/8 inch) cubes

100 g (3^{1}/2 oz) baby bok choy (pak choi), roughly shredded

1 tablespoon lime juice

2 tablespoons coriander (cilantro) leaves

ASIAN NOODLE SOUP

4 dried Chinese mushrooms

50 g (1³/₄ oz) dried rice vermicelli

400 g (14 oz) Chinese broccoli, cut into 5 cm (2 inch) lengths

4 fried tofu puffs, cut into strips

60 g (2¹/₄ oz) bean sprouts

500 ml (17 fl oz/2 cups) vegetable stock

1 tablespoon light soy sauce

2 teaspoons Chinese rice wine

1¹/₂ spring onions (scallions), finely chopped

coriander (cilantro) leaves, to serve

Place the dried mushrooms in a bowl, cover with boiling water and soak for 15 minutes. Drain, reserving 60 ml (2 fl oz/¹/₄ cup) of the liquid. Squeeze the mushrooms to remove any excess liquid. Discard the stems and thinly slice the caps.

Soak the vermicelli in boiling water for 5 minutes. Drain. Divide the vermicelli, broccoli, tofu puffs and bean sprouts among the two serving bowls.

Place the reserved mushroom liquid, stock, soy sauce, rice wine, spring onion and mushrooms in a saucepan and bring to the boil. Cook, covered, for 10 minutes.

Ladle the soup into the serving bowls and garnish with the coriander leaves.

REALLY EASY! | 25 MINUTES | SERVES 2 | VEGAN

SWEET POTATO AND PEAR SOUP

Food processors and blenders are now widely available and an inexpensive addition to any student kitchen. They make life so much easier but if you don't have one to hand a good old-fashioned fork will do.

Melt the butter in a saucepan over medium heat, add the onion and cook for 2–3 minutes, or until softened but not brown. Add the sweet potato and pear, and cook, stirring, for 1–2 minutes. Add the stock to the pan, bring to the boil and cook for 20 minutes, or until the sweet potato and pear are soft.

Cool slightly, then place the mixture in a blender or food processor and blend in batches until smooth. Return to the pan, stir in the cream and gently reheat without boiling. Season with salt and ground black pepper. Garnish with the mint.

15 g ($^{1}/_{2}$ oz) butter

$^{1}/_{2}$ small white onion, finely chopped

375 g (13 oz) orange sweet potato, peeled and cut into 2 cm ($^{3}/_{4}$ inch) dice

1 firm pear (250 g/9 oz), peeled, cored and cut into 2 cm ($^{3}/_{4}$ inch) dice

375 ml (13 fl oz/1$^{1}/_{2}$ cups) vegetable stock

125 ml (4 fl oz/$^{1}/_{2}$ cup) cream

mint leaves, to garnish

MUSHROOM AND TORTELLINI SOUP

½ tablespoon olive oil

60 g (2¼ oz) small flat mushrooms, sliced

3 spring onions (scallions), sliced

½ small garlic clove, crushed

600 ml (21 fl oz/2½ cups) vegetable stock

½ tablespoon port

1 teaspoon Worcestershire sauce

100 g (3½ oz) fresh large ricotta tortellini

shaved parmesan cheese, to garnish

This is one of my favourite soups but make sure that the Worcestershire sauce is the vegetarian kind!

Heat the oil in a large heavy-based saucepan. Add the mushrooms and cook over high heat for 2 minutes, browning the mushrooms before turning. Add the spring onion and garlic and cook for a further 1 minute.

Meanwhile, **bring** the stock to the boil in a separate saucepan. Add the stock, port and Worcestershire sauce to the mushroom mixture and bring to the boil. Add the tortellini and simmer for 8 minutes, or until the tortellini is *al dente*.

Season the soup with salt and cracked black pepper to taste and serve topped with shaved parmesan.

REALLY EASY! 25 MINUTES SERVES 2

SPRING VEGETABLE SOUP WITH BASIL PESTO

Home-made pesto or fresh pesto from a deli will really add an edge to this recipe but if you really don't have the money or the time then a bottled pesto will do just fine If you prefer a thinner pesto, mix it with a little olive oil to give it a runnier consistency.

Bring the stock to the boil in a large saucepan. Meanwhile, heat the olive oil in a large heavy-based saucepan and add the spring onion and celery. Cover and cook over medium heat for 5 minutes, or until softened.

Add the stock to the spring onion mixture and mix well. Add the carrot, asparagus and corn to the pan. Return the mixture to the boil, then reduce the heat and simmer for 10 minutes.

Spoon into warmed soup bowls. Top with a dollop of pesto, season to taste with salt and pepper, and garnish with shaved parmesan.

REALLY EASY! | 30 MINUTES | SERVES 2

600 ml (21 fl oz/2$^{1}/_{2}$ cups) vegetable stock

$^{1}/_{2}$ tablespoon extra virgin olive oil

4 spring onions (scallions), finely sliced

1 celery stalk, finely sliced

6 baby (dutch) carrots, sliced

155 g (1 bunch) asparagus, woody ends removed, cut into 3 cm (1$^{1}/_{4}$ inch) lengths

75 g (2$^{1}/_{2}$ oz) baby corn, cut into 3 cm (1$^{1}/_{4}$ inch) lengths

2 teaspoons fresh or bottled pesto

extra virgin olive oil, to thin pesto

shaved parmesan cheese, to garnish

VEGETABLE AND LENTIL SOUP WITH SPICED YOGHURT

1 tablespoon olive oil

1/2 leek, white part only, chopped

1 garlic clove, crushed

1 teaspoon curry powder

1/2 teaspoon ground cumin

1/2 teaspoon garam masala

375 ml (13 fl oz/1 1/2 cups) vegetable stock

1 bay leaf

60 g (2 1/4 oz) brown lentils

150 g (5 1/2 oz) butternut pumpkin (squash), peeled and cut into 1 cm (1/2 inch) cubes

1 small courgette (zucchini), cut in half lengthways and sliced

135 g (4 3/4 oz) tin chopped tomatoes

70 g (2 1/2 oz) broccoli, cut into small florets

1/2 small carrot, diced

30 g (1 oz) peas

Heat the oil in a saucepan over medium heat. Add the leek and garlic and cook for 4–5 minutes, or until soft and lightly golden. Add the curry powder, cumin and garam masala and cook for 1 minute, or until fragrant.

Add the stock, bay leaf, lentils and pumpkin. Bring to the boil, then reduce the heat to low and simmer for 10–15 minutes, or until the lentils are tender. Season well.

Add the courgette, tomato, broccoli, carrot and 170 ml (5 1/2 fl oz/2/3 cup) water and simmer for 10 minutes, or until the vegetables are tender. Add the peas and simmer for 2–3 minutes.

Dollop a spoonful of yoghurt on each serving of soup.

EASY!   **50** MINUTES   SERVES **2**

TOMATO AND PASTA SOUP

This tasty soup will soon become one of your staples that you will cook time and time again! If you want to give this soup a slightly different flavour, serve with a dollop of fresh pesto.

Place the stock in a heavy-based saucepan and bring to the boil. Reduce the heat, add the pasta, carrot and courgette and cook for about 5–10 minutes, or until the pasta is *al dente*.

Add the tomato and heat through gently for a few more minutes. Season to taste.

Pour the soup into warm soup bowls and sprinkle the basil over the top. Serve with a fresh wholemeal loaf.

625 ml (21^1/$_2$ fl oz/2^1/$_2$ cups) vegetable stock

45 g (1^3/$_4$ oz/^{1}/$_2$ cup) spiral pasta

1 carrot, sliced

^{1}/$_2$ courgette (zucchini), sliced

2 ripe tomatoes, roughly chopped

1 tablespoon shredded basil

fresh wholemeal loaf, to serve

BROTH WITH RAVIOLI

750 ml (26 fl oz/3 cups)
vegetable stock

250 g (9 oz) spinach
and ricotta ravioli

85 g (3 oz) snow peas
(mangetout), sliced
on the diagonal

2 tablespoons chopped
flat-leaf (Italian) parsley

2 tablespoons
chopped basil

grated parmesan cheese,
to garnish

This is so easy and one of the recipes that I relied on time and time again during my years at college. It is so simple to make, stores well and is healthy and filling. Perfect for those colder days when you need warming from the inside out.

Place the stock in a large heavy-based saucepan and bring to the boil. Add the ravioli and cook for 8–10 minutes, or until the pasta is *al dente*.

Season to taste with salt and pepper, and stir in the snowpeas, parsley and basil. Pour the soup into two bowls and sprinkle with grated parmesan before serving.

REALLY EASY!

20 MINUTES

SERVES **2**

COURGETTE PESTO SOUP

I love to serve this soup with toasted ciabatta bread but it tastes just as good if served with toasted sliced white.

Heat the oil in a large heavy-based saucepan. Add the onion and garlic and cook over medium heat for 5 minutes, or until the onion is soft.

Bring the stock to the boil in a separate saucepan. Add the courgette and hot stock to the onion mixture. Bring to the boil, then reduce the heat, cover and simmer for about 10 minutes, or until the courgette is very soft.

Transfer the courgette mixture to a blender or food processor and blend in batches until smooth. Return the mixture to the pan, stir in the cream and 1 tablespoon of the pesto, and reheat over medium heat until hot. Season with salt and black pepper and serve with toasted ciabatta bread and the remaining pesto.

REALLY EASY!

30 MINUTES

SERVES 2

$^1\!/_2$ tablespoon olive oil

$^1\!/_2$ onion, finely chopped

1 garlic clove, crushed

375 ml (13 fl oz/1$^1\!/_2$ cups) vegetable stock

375 g (13 oz) zucchini (courgettes), thinly sliced

30 ml (2 fl oz) cream

2 tablespoons fresh or bottled pesto

toasted ciabatta bread, to serve

MISO SOUP WITH UDON AND TOFU

1 teaspoon dashi granules

3 tablespoons red (genmai) miso

2 tablespoons soy sauce

400 g (14 oz) fresh udon noodles, separated

400 g (14 oz) silken firm tofu, cubed

100 g (3½ oz) fresh shiitake mushrooms, sliced

500 g (1 bunch) baby bok choy (pak choi), leaves separated

Dashi is a fish stock made from kelp and dried bonito flakes. Adding another strange ingredient to your store cupboard may seem like a waste of money but these granules pack a healthy punch and are well worth the investment. They will last for many months and add a delicious flavour to this soup.

Place the dashi, miso, soy sauce and 1.25 litres (44 fl oz/5 cups) water in a large saucepan and bring to the boil. Reduce the heat and simmer for 10 minutes.

Add the udon noodles and cook for 5 minutes, or until soft. Stir in the tofu, shiitake mushrooms and bok choy and cook for 3 minutes, or until the bok choy wilts.

REALLY EASY! · 30 MINUTES · SERVES 2 · VEGAN

SAFFRON AND JERUSALEM ARTICHOKE SOUP

Place the saffron threads in a bowl with 2 tablespoons boiling water and leave until needed. Peel and thinly slice the artichokes, dropping the slices into a bowl of water mixed with lemon juice to prevent discolouration.

Heat the oil in a large heavy-based saucepan, add the onion and cook over medium heat for 2–3 minutes, or until the onion is softened. Bring the stock to the boil in a separate saucepan. Add the cumin to the onion mixture and cook for a further 30 seconds, or until fragrant. Add the drained artichokes, potato, saffron mixture, stock and extra lemon juice. Bring to the boil, then reduce the heat and simmer for 15–18 minutes, or until the artichokes are very soft.

Transfer to a blender and process in batches until smooth. Return the soup to the pan and season to taste with salt and cracked pepper. Reheat over medium heat and serve.

1 pinch saffron threads

125 g (4$^{1}/_{2}$ oz) Jerusalem artichokes

1 tablespoon lemon juice

$^{1}/_{2}$ tablespoon olive oil

$^{1}/_{2}$ onion, finely chopped

500 ml (17 fl oz/2 cups) vegetable stock

1$^{1}/_{2}$ teaspoons ground cumin

250 g (9 oz) desiree potatoes, grated

$^{1}/_{2}$ teaspoon lemon juice, extra

REALLY EASY! · 35 MINUTES · SERVES 2 · VEGAN

SWEET POTATO SOUP

½ tablespoon
vegetable oil

1 small onion, chopped

2 garlic cloves, crushed

1 teaspoon grated
fresh ginger

½ tablespoon Madras
curry powder

500 g (1 lb 2 oz) orange
sweet potato, peeled and
chopped into 5 cm
(2 inch) chunks

500 ml (17 fl oz/
2 cups) vegetable stock

200 ml (7 fl oz)
coconut milk

small handful coriander
(cilantro) leaves,
chopped

fried Asian shallots
and naan bread or
chappati, to serve

Just serving some sliced bread alongside this soup turns it from a snack into a meal. I always like to eat this particular soup with generous wedges of heated naan bread or chappati, but frankly any bread will clean up the bowl just as well! Fried onion flakes are available from Asian food stores.

Heat the oil in a large saucepan. Add the onion and cook over medium heat for 3 minutes, or until softened. Add the garlic, ginger and curry powder. Stir for a further 1 minute. Add the sweet potato and stir to coat in the mixture.

Pour over the stock. Bring to the boil then lower the heat. Cover and simmer for 20 minutes, or until the sweet potato is cooked.

Cool slightly, then process in batches, using a food processor, until smooth. Return to the saucepan and stir in the coconut milk and coriander, reserving some coriander for garnish. Stir and reheat for 2–3 minutes. Serve in bowls topped with a sprinkle of fried Asian shallots and the remaining coriander. Serve with heated naan bread or chappati.

REALLY EASY! · 50 MINUTES · SERVES 2 · VEGAN

POTATO AND ROCKET SOUP

This is another easy soup to make which you can leave simmering away in the background while you address more pressing student matters!

Place the stock in a large heavy-based saucepan and bring to the boil. Add the potato and garlic and simmer over medium heat for 15 minutes, or until the potato is tender to the point of a sharp knife. Add the rocket and simmer for a further 2 minutes. Stir in the olive oil.

Transfer the mixture to a blender or food processor and blend in batches until smooth. Return the mixture to the pan and stir over medium heat until hot. Season to taste with salt and cracked black pepper and serve in warmed bowls. Garnish with the rocket leaves and shaved parmesan before serving.

REALLY EASY! **30 MINUTES** **SERVES 2** **VEGAN**

500 ml (17 fl oz/2 cups) vegetable stock

400 g (14 oz) desiree potatoes, chopped into small pieces

1 garlic clove, peeled, left whole

85 g (3 oz) rocket (arugula)

2 teaspoons extra virgin olive oil

extra rocket (arugula) leaves, to garnish (optional)

2 tablespoons shaved parmesan cheese (optional)

PASTA AND NOODLES

INTRODUCTION

Pasta is one of the most easily prepared, versatile and filling ingredients you can buy. It is high in protein, low in sodium and fat, contains vitamins, iron, minerals, fibre and uses no preservatives. Whether it is simply boiled and served with a splash of olive oil and garlic or formed into a more intricate baked dish, it is never boring.

Pasta is simply hard flour blended into a firm dough with water and eggs. It is fairly easy to make fresh pasta yourself but it is time-consuming. When there are so many varieties of pasta you can buy cheaply and cook in a few minutes, opt for dried or ready-made fresh pasta.

Pasta comes in an array of shapes and sizes, which can sometimes be confusing, However, many shapes are interchangeable. Thin, long pasta needs a good clinging sauce; hollow or twisted shapes take chunky sauces; wide, flat noodles need rich sauces; and delicate shapes require a light sauce without large pieces in it.

Noodles are a type of pasta made from flour, water and sometimes egg, the word noodle can be used to describe hundreds of different types used in cuisines around the world. Noodles are important to Asian cuisine, especially to China and Japan, and long egg noodles are eaten with stews in Eastern Europe. Japanese noodles are not made from rice, as it is too precious a commodity. Instead they are made from buckwheat and/or wheat.

Choose noodles that are appropriate to the recipe if they are not specified exactly. Thin, delicate rice vermicelli will soak up Vietnamese flavours well but thick egg noodles won't. Noodles for use in soups must be robust enough to pick up without breaking and falling back into the soup. Noodles can now be bought pre-cooked to various stages.

SPAGHETTI WITH HERBS AND TOMATO

10 g (⅓ oz) fresh breadcrumbs

250 g (9 oz) spaghetti

30 ml (1 fl oz) olive oil

1 garlic clove, diced

15 g (½ oz) chopped herbs (such as basil, coriander, parsley)

2 tomatoes, chopped

15 g (½ oz) chopped walnuts

15 g (½ oz) grated parmesan cheese, plus extra, to serve

Walnuts are a favourite of mine but you can omit them from this recipe without any real loss of taste.

Heat the grill (broiler) to medium and put the fresh breadcrumbs under for a few seconds, or until slightly golden.

Cook the spaghetti in a saucepan of rapidly boiling salted water until *al dente*, then drain.

Heat 2 tablespoons of the olive oil in a large frying pan and cook the garlic until soft. Add the remaining oil and the herbs, tomato, walnuts and parmesan. Add the cooked pasta to the pan and toss for 1–2 minutes. Top with the breadcrumbs and extra parmesan.

REALLY EASY! · 35 MINUTES · SERVES 2

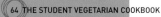

RAVIOLI
WITH ROASTED RED CAPSICUM SAUCE

Cut the peppers into large pieces, removing the seeds and membrane. Cook, skin-side up, under a hot grill (broiler) until the skin blackens and blisters. Cool in a plastic bag, then peel away the skin.

Cook the pasta in a large saucepan of boiling water until *al dente*.

Meanwhile, **heat** the olive oil in a frying pan and cook the garlic and leek over medium heat for 3–4 minutes, or until softened. Add the oregano and brown sugar and stir for 1 minute.

Place the pepper and leek mixture in a food processor or blender, season with salt and pepper and process until combined. Add the stock and process until smooth. Drain the pasta and return to the saucepan. Gently toss the sauce through the ravioli over low heat until warmed through. Divide among two serving bowls and serve immediately.

3 red peppers (capsicums)

310 g (11 oz) ravioli

1 tablespoon olive oil

1 garlic clove, crushed

1 leek, thinly sliced

$1/2$ tablespoon chopped oregano

1 teaspoon soft brown sugar

125 ml ($1/2$ cup) hot vegetable stock

REALLY EASY!

40 MINUTES

SERVES **2**

FETTUCINE WITH CREAMY SPINACH AND ROAST TOMATO

3 roma (plum) tomatoes

20 g (³/₄ oz) butter

1 garlic clove, crushed

¹/₂ onion, chopped

225 g (8 oz) English spinach, trimmed

125 ml (4 fl oz/¹/₂ cup) vegetable stock

60 ml (¹/₄ cup) thick (double/heavy) cream

225 g (8 oz) fresh spinach fettucine

25 g (1 oz) shaved Parmesan cheese

I still cook this dish several times a month even though my student days are well behind me. I think it is the taste and smell of the roast tomatoes which keep me coming back to it.

Preheat the oven to 220°C (425°F/Gas 7). Cut the tomatoes in half lengthways, then cut each half into three wedges. Place the wedges on a lightly greased baking tray and bake for 30–35 minutes, or until softened and slightly golden.

Meanwhile, **heat** the butter in a large frying pan. Add the garlic and onion and cook over medium heat for 5 minutes, or until the onion is soft. Add the spinach, stock and cream, increase the heat to high and bring to the boil. Simmer rapidly for 5 minutes.

While the spinach mixture is cooking, **cook** the pasta in a large saucepan of boiling water until *al dente*. Drain and return to the pan. Remove the spinach mixture from the heat and season well. Cool slightly, then process in a food processor until smooth. Toss through the pasta until well coated. Divide among serving bowls, top with the roasted tomatoes and parmesan shavings, and serve.

REALLY EASY!

40 MINUTES

SERVES **2**

FREEFORM PUMPKIN, SPINACH AND RICOTTA LASAGNE

This really is an impressive dish and so filling too!

Heat the oil in a non-stick frying pan over medium heat. Add the pumpkin and toss. Cook, stirring occasionally, for 15 minutes, or until tender (don't worry if the pumpkin is slightly mashed). Season and keep warm.

Cook the spinach in a large saucepan of boiling water for 30 seconds, or until wilted. Using a slotted spoon, transfer to a bowl of cold water. Drain well and squeeze out as much excess water as possible. Finely chop the spinach. Add the lasagne sheets to the pan of boiling water and cook, stirring occasionally, until *al dente*. Drain and lay the sheets side-by-side on a clean tea towel. Cut each sheet widthways into thirds.

Put the ricotta, cream, parmesan, spinach and nutmeg in a small pan. Stir over low heat for 2–3 minutes, or until warmed through. Work quickly to assemble. Place a piece of lasagne on the base of each plate. Using half the pumpkin, top each of the sheets, then cover with another piece of lasagne. Use half the ricotta mixture to spread over the lasagne sheets, then add another lasagne piece.

Top with the remaining pumpkin, then remaining ricotta mixture. Season well and serve immediately.

30 ml (1 fl oz) olive oil

750 g (1 lb 10 oz) butternut pumpkin (squash), cut into 1.5 cm (5/8 inch) dice

250 g (9 oz) English spinach leaves, thoroughly washed

2 fresh lasagne sheets (12 x 20 cm/ 5 x 8 inches)

250 g (9 oz/1cup) ricotta cheese

1 tablespoon cream

15 g (1/2 oz) grated Parmesan cheese

pinch ground nutmeg

REALLY EASY! **35** MINUTES SERVES **2**

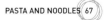

CASARECCI PASTA
WITH ROASTED TOMATOES, ROCKET AND GOAT'S CHEESE

200 g (7 oz) casarecci pasta

40 ml (1¼ fl oz) olive oil

1 garlic clove, finely sliced

60 g (2¼ oz) semi-dried (sunblush) tomatoes

1 tablespoon lemon juice

60 g (2¼ oz/2 cups) rocket (arugula), roughly chopped

1 tablespoon chopped parsley

18 g (¾ oz) grated parmesan cheese

50 g (1¾ oz) goat's cheese

Casarecci pasta looks like a small tube that has been gently twisted. Each piece is normally 5mm long with a slit along the back. Fusilli pasta is a great substitute if you don't want to go the bother of finding this particular one.

In a large saucepan of boiling salted water, **cook** the pasta until *al dente*. Drain and keep warm.

Heat the olive oil and garlic over low–medium heat until it just begins to sizzle. Remove immediately, and add to the pasta with the tomatoes, lemon juice, rocket, parsley and parmesan. Stir gently to combine, allowing the heat from the pasta to wilt the rocket. Serve topped with crumbled goat's cheese.

REALLY EASY! · 20 MINUTES · SERVES 2

FUSILLI WITH BROCCOLINI, CHILLI AND OLIVES

Fusilli pasta is one of the most popular pasta shapes. It's distinctive spiral shape ensures it absorbs and retains the flavours around it.

Heat the olive oil in a large non-stick frying pan over medium heat. Cook the onion, garlic and chilli until softened, then add the broccolini and cook for 5 minutes. Pour in the stock and cook, covered, for 5 minutes.

Meanwhile, **cook** the fusilli in a large saucepan of rapidly boiling water until *al dente*. Drain and keep warm.

When the broccolini is tender, **remove** from the heat. Add to the pasta with the olives, parsley, pecorino and basil, and season well. Gently toss together and serve immediately.

REALLY EASY! 25 MINUTES SERVES 2

1 1/2 tablespoons olive oil

1/2 onion, finely chopped

1 garlic clove chopped

1/2 teaspoon chilli flakes

350 g (12 oz) broccolini, cut into 1 cm (1/2 inch) pieces

60 ml (2 fl oz/1/4 cup) vegetable stock

200 g (7 oz) fusilli pasta

45 g (1 1/2 oz/1/4 cup) black olives, pitted and chopped

1 tablespoon finely chopped parsley

15 g (1/2 oz) grated pecorino cheese

1 tablespoon basil leaves, shredded

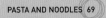

BALSAMIC PEPPER ON ANGEL HAIR

150 g (5¼ oz) angel hair pasta

---

1 red pepper (capsicum)

---

1 yellow pepper (capsicum)

---

1 green pepper (capsicum)

---

2 garlic cloves, crushed

---

1 tablespoon orange juice

---

40 ml (1¼ oz) balsamic vinegar

---

50 g (1¾ oz) goat's cheese

---

2 tablespoons basil

Don't be put off by the need for goat's cheese! This is a really tasty meal and even if your finances dictate that you can't enjoy this recipe as frequently as you would like, it is just perfect for those special occasions.

Cook the pasta in a large saucepan of rapidly boiling water until *al dente*. Drain well.

Cut the peppers into large flat pieces and place under a hot grill (broiler) until the skins blister and blacken. Leave to cool in a plastic bag, then peel away the skin and cut the flesh into thin strips.

Combine the pepper strips, garlic, orange juice and balsamic vinegar. Drizzle over the pasta and gently toss.

Serve topped with crumbled goat's cheese and basil and a sprinkling of cracked black pepper.

REALLY EASY! | 25 MINUTES | SERVES 2

SPAGHETTI WITH LEMON AND ROCKET

I am always making this dish but sometimes I prefer to substitute basil leaves for the rocket. It gives the spaghetti a really fresh taste. Leave out the parmesan if you are looking for a vegan option.

Cook the spaghetti according to the packet instructions until *al dente*. Drain well.

Combine the rocket, lemon zest, garlic, chilli, chilli oil, extra virgin olive oil and two-thirds of the grated parmesan in a large bowl and mix together gently.

Add the pasta to the rocket and lemon mixture and stir together well. Serve topped with the remaining parmesan and season to taste with salt and cracked black pepper.

REALLY EASY! · 20 MINUTES · SERVES 2 · VEGAN

180 g (6^1/$_2$ oz) spaghetti

50 g (1^3/$_4$ oz) rocket (arugula), finely shredded

^{1}/$_2$ tablespoon finely chopped lemon zest

^{1}/$_2$ garlic clove, finely chopped

^{1}/$_2$ small red chilli, seeded and finely chopped

^{1}/$_2$ teaspoon chilli oil

2^1/$_2$ tablespoons extra virgin olive oil

30 g (1 oz) parmesan cheese, finely grated (optional)

FUSILLI WITH ROASTED TOMATOES, TAPENADE AND BOCCONCINI

400 g (14 oz) cherry
or teardrop tomatoes
(or a mixture of both),
halved if they are large

250 g (9 oz) fusilli

150 g (5^1/$_2$ oz) baby
bocconcini cheese, sliced

^{1}/$_2$ tablespoon
chopped thyme

2 tablespoons fresh
or bottled tapenade

I think everyone now knows that *al dente* means 'just firm to the bite'. Fewer people know that when adding the pasta to the pot of boiling water you should only stir once or you risk the pasta breaking up.

Preheat the oven to 200°C (400°F/Gas 6). Place the tomatoes on a baking tray, sprinkle with salt and pepper and bake for 10 minutes, or until slightly dried.

Cook the pasta in a large saucepan of rapidly boiling water until *al dente*, then drain.

Toss the tapenade and bocconcini through the hot pasta. Top with the roasted tomatoes and thyme and serve immediately.

REALLY EASY!   15 MINUTES   SERVES 2

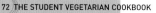

ORECCHIETTE WITH BROCCOLI

Orecchiette means 'little ears' and their curved saucer-shape and rough texture makes them ideal for holding sauce.

Blanch the broccoli in a saucepan of boiling salted water for 5 minutes, or until just tender. Remove with a slotted spoon, drain well and return the water to the boil. Cook the pasta in the boiling water until *al dente*, then drain well and return to the pan.

Meanwhile, **heat** the oil in a heavy-based frying pan and add the chilli flakes and broccoli. Increase the heat to medium and cook, stirring, for 5 minutes, or until the broccoli is well coated and beginning to break apart. Season. Add to the pasta, toss in the cheese and serve.

REALLY EASY! **20** MINUTES SERVES **2** VEGAN

375 g (13 oz) broccoli, cut into florets

225 g (8 oz) orecchiette

30 ml (1 fl oz) extra virgin olive oil

¼ teaspoon dried chilli flakes

15 g (1½ oz) grated pecorino or parmesan cheese (optional)

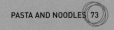

BUCATINI WITH FARMHOUSE SAUCE

1 tablespoon olive oil

125 g (4 ½ oz) mushrooms

½ medium aubergine (eggplant) cut into cubes

1 garlic clove , crushed

415 g (14¾ oz) tinned chopped tomatoes

250 g (9 oz) bucatini or spaghetti

salt and pepper

1½ tablespoons chopped fresh parsley

The only problem I have ever encountered with this lovely dish is that sometimes I manage to cook the pasta before I am ready to serve it. The pasta then starts to stick together creating a huge pasta ball! If this happens to you add a little olive oil after draining and toss the oil through the pasta.

Heat the olive oil in a medium heavy-based pan. Wipe the mushrooms with paper towels and then slice them. Add the mushrooms, cubes of aubergine and the garlic to the pan and cook, stirring, for 4 minutes. Add the undrained, chopped tomatoes; cover the pan and simmer for 15 minutes.

While the sauce is cooking, **add** the pasta to a large pan of rapidly boiling water and cook until just tender. Drain the pasta well and then return it to the pan. Season the sauce with salt and pepper. Add the chopped parsley to the pan and stir through. Add the sauce to the pasta and toss until well distributed. Serve immediately in warmed pasta bowls.

REALLY EASY!

35 MINUTES

SERVES **2**

VEGAN

SPAGHETTI WITH FRESH TOMATO SAUCE

If you have a nice health basil plant growing on a sunny shelf in your kitchen you may want to try a slight variation to this recipe. Simply add an additional large handful of fresh basil leaves to the mixture. It really adds another level of freshness to this simple dish.

Chop the spring onions finely. Cut the tomatoes into small pieces. Chop the olives and capers. Place all ingredients, except pasta, in a bowl; mix well. Cover and refrigerate for at least 2 hours.

Add the pasta to a large pan of rapidly boiling water and cook until tender. Drain the pasta and return it to the pan.

Add the cold sauce to the hot pasta and mix well.

2 spring onions

2 firm, ripe tomatoes

4 stuffed green olives

1 tablespoon capers

1 garlic clove, crushed

$1/4$ teaspoon dried oregano

2 tablespoons chopped fresh parsley

40 ml (1 $1/4$ fl oz) olive oil

250 g (8 oz) thin spaghetti

REALLY EASY!

20 MINUTES + COOLING TIME

SERVES **2**

VEGAN

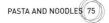

PUMPKIN AND PINE NUT TAGLIATELLE

½ large onion

375 g (13 oz) butternut pumpkin (squash)

15 g (½ oz) butter

1 garlic clove, crushed

180 ml (6 fl oz/¾ cup) vegetable stock

teaspoon ground nutmeg

125 ml (4 fl oz/½ cup) pouring (whipping) cream

250 g (9 oz) fresh tagliatelle

40 g (1½ oz/¼ cup) pine nuts, toasted

1 tablespoon snipped chives

freshly grated parmesan cheese, to serve

Be sure to toast the pine nuts in a dry frying pan over medium heat, stirring constantly, until they are golden brown and fragrant. But keep watch very carefully as they will burn easily and you don't want the local fire brigade turning up and asking for the recipe!

Chop the onion. Chop the pumpkin into small pieces. Melt the butter in a large saucepan. Add the onion and cook for 3 minutes, or until soft and golden. Add the garlic and cook for another minute. Stir in the vegetable stock and add the pumpkin. Bring to the boil, reduce the heat slightly and cook until the pumpkin is tender. Reduce the heat to very low and season with the nutmeg and ½ teaspoon black pepper. Stir in the cream until just warmed through — do not boil. Cool slightlyTransfer to a food processor and process for about 30 seconds, until the mixture forms a smooth sauce.

Meanwhile, **cook** the tagliatelle in a large saucepan of rapidly boiling salted water until *al dente*. Drain and return to the pan. Return the sauce to the pan and gently reheat. Add to the pasta with the pine nuts and toss well. Serve sprinkled with chives and parmesan.

REALLY EASY! 50 MINUTES SERVES 2

TORTELLINI WITH AUBERGINE

This is such a tasty recipe but remember to cut the eggplant just before using, as it turns brown when exposed to the air.

Cut the red pepper in half, remove the seeds and membrane and cut into small squares. Cut the aubergine into small cubes.

Cook the tortellini in a large saucepan of rapidly boiling salted water until *al dente*. Drain and return to the pan.

While the pasta is cooking, **heat** the oil in a large frying pan, add the garlic and red pepper and stir over medium heat for 1 minute. Add the aubergine to the pan and stir gently over medium heat for 5 minutes, or until lightly browned.

Add the undrained tomatoes and vegetable stock to the pan. Stir and bring to the boil. Reduce the heat to low, cover the pan and cook for 10 minutes, or until the vegetables are tender. Add the basil and pasta and stir until mixed through.

REALLY EASY! · 30 MINUTES · SERVES 2

$1/2$ red pepper (capsicum)

250 g (9 oz) aubergine (eggplant)

250 g (9 oz) fresh cheese and spinach tortellini

30 ml (1 fl oz) oil

1 garlic clove, crushed

210 g ($7^1/2$ oz) tinned chopped tomatoes

125 ml (4 fl oz) vegetable stock

15 g ($1/2$ oz) chopped basil

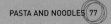

LINGUINE
WITH ROASTED VEGETABLE SAUCE

2 large red peppers (capsicums)

250 g (9 oz) firm ripe tomatoes

1 large red onion

$^1/_2$ bulb garlic

60 ml (2 fl oz/$^1/_4$ cup) balsamic vinegar

30 ml (1 fl oz) olive oil

1 teaspoon sea salt

1 teaspoon freshly ground black pepper

250 g (9 oz) linguine

50 g (1$^3/_4$ oz) parmesan cheese, shaved

50 g (1$^3/_4$ oz) black olives

This isn't the quickest pasta recipe around but if you stick with it you will be rewarded with a dish of subtle flavours and sauce to die for!

Preheat the oven to 180°C (350°F/Gas 4). Cut the peppers in half and remove the seeds and membrane. Cut the tomatoes and onions in half and separate and peel the garlic cloves.

Arrange the vegetables in a large ovenproof dish in a single layer. Pour the vinegar and oil over them and sprinkle with the sea salt and pepper. Bake for 50 minutes. Allow to cool for 5 minutes before puréeing in a food processor for 3 minutes, or until the mixture is smooth. Season with more salt and pepper, if necessary.

When the vegetables are almost cooked, **cook** the linguine in a large saucepan of rapidly boiling salted water until *al dente*. Drain. Serve the roasted vegetable sauce over the linguine with the parmesan cheese, olives and some extra black pepper.

REALLY EASY! · 80 MINUTES · SERVES 2

SPAGHETTI WITH PRIMAVERA SAUCE

This is the perfect recipe for using up any vegetables you have found in the bottom of the basket. You can use leeks, courgettes and sugar snap peas, and add some fresh chopped dill or basil if you like.

Add the spaghetti to a pan of rapidly boiling water and cook until just tender. Drain and return to the pan.

While the spaghetti is cooking, **cut** the asparagus into small pieces. Bring a medium pan of water to the boil, add the asparagus and cook for 2 minutes. Using a slotted spoon, remove from pan and plunge into cold water.

Plunge the broad beans into a pan of boiling water. Remove at once and cool in cold water. Drain and allow to cool completely. Peel the skin from the beans.

Heat the butter in a heavy-based frying pan. Add the celery and stir for 2 minutes. Add the peas and cream and cook for another 3 minutes. Add the asparagus, broad beans, parmesan, salt and pepper and bring to the boil; cook for 1 minute. Add the sauce to the spaghetti and toss to combine. Serve spaghetti immediately in warmed pasta bowls.

250 g (9 oz) spaghetti

75 g (2$^{1}/_{2}$ oz) fresh asparagus

180 g (6$^{1}/_{2}$ oz/$^{1}/_{2}$ cup) frozen broad beans

20 g ($^{3}/_{4}$ oz) butter

$^{1}/_{2}$ celery stick, sliced

75 g (2$^{1}/_{2}$ oz) frozen green peas

155 ml (5 fl oz) cream

25 g (1 oz) freshly grated parmesan cheese

salt and pepper

REALLY EASY! 40 MINUTES SERVES 2

PENNE WITH TOMATO AND ONION JAM WITH OLIVES

30 ml (1 fl oz) olive oil

2 red onions, sliced

1/2 tablespoon soft brown sugar

1 tablespoon balsamic vinegar

1 x 400 g (14 oz) tin tomatoes

250 g (9 oz) penne rigate

75 g (2 1/2 oz) small pitted black olives or pitted and halved Kalamata olives

35 g (1 1/4 oz/1/3 cup) grated Parmesan cheese

This isn't a dish to whip-up after a long day of study but it's perfect for those long summer evenings when your work load isn't too onerous. The caramelised onions will keep in the fridge for a couple of days and you can always use them as a pizza topping.

Heat the oil in a non-stick frying pan over medium heat. Add the onion and sugar and cook for 25–30 minutes, or until caramelised.

Stir in the vinegar, bring to the boil and cook for 5 minutes. Add the tomatoes, return to the boil, then reduce the heat to medium–low and simmer for 25 minutes, or until the tomatoes are reduced and jam-like.

Cook the pasta in a large saucepan of rapidly boiling salted water according to the packet instructions until *al dente*. Drain, then return to the pan. Add the tomato mixture and olives and stir to combine well. Season to taste with salt and black pepper and garnish with the grated parmesan.

REALLY EASY!

70 MINUTES

SERVES 2

SPAGHETTI SIRACUSANI

So called because of its Sicilian origins this dish is a low-fat favourite of mine. Omit the parmesan cheese for a great vegan option.

Remove membrane and seeds from green pepper. Slice into thin strips. Heat oil in a large, deep pan. Add garlic, stir for 30 seconds over low heat. Add pepper strips, undrained chopped tomatoes, water, courgettes, capers and olives. Cook for 20 minutes, stirring occasionally.

Add basil, salt and pepper, stir. Meanwhile, add pasta to a large pan of rapidly boiling water; cook until just tender; drain. Serve in warmed bowls, top with sauce and sprinkle with parmesan.

REALLY EASY! · 45 MINUTES · SERVES 2 · VEGAN

½ large green pepper (capsicum)

1 tablespoon olive oil

1 garlic clove, crushed

1 x 425 g (15 oz) tin tomatoes

60 ml (2 fl oz) water

1 medium courgette (zucchini), chopped

½ tablespoon capers, chopped

1½ tablespoons black olives, pitted and halved

1 handful chopped fresh basil leaves

salt and pepper

250 g (9 oz) spaghetti or linguine

25 g (¾ oz) freshly grated parmesan cheese, for serving (optional)

ROASTED VEGETABLE LASAGNE

Marinade

125 ml (4 fl oz/^{1}/$_2$ cup) olive oil

2 tablespoons red wine vinegar

1 tablespoon finely chopped capers

1 tablespoon finely chopped parsley

1 garlic clove , finely chopped

1 teaspoon tomato paste

salt and pepper

1 red pepper (capsicum)

1 large aubergine (eggplant), sliced lengthways, salted, rinsed and well-drained

2 large courgettes (zucchinis), sliced thinly lengthways

400 g (14 oz) sweet potato, peeled and sliced thinly lengthways

6 plum (roma) tomatoes, quartered

375 g (13 oz) fresh lasagne sheets

90 g (3 oz/^{1}/$_3$ cup) good-quality pesto

300 g (10^1/$_2$ oz) bocconcini, finely sliced

olive oil

100 g (3^1/$_3$ oz/1 cup) freshly grated Parmesan cheese

Preheat the oven to moderately hot 200°C (400°F/Gas). Combine marinade ingredients in a non-metalic bowl and whisk thoroughly.

Cut red pepper in half lengthways. Remove seeds and membrane and cut into large, flattish pieces. Grill until skin blackens and blisters. Place on a cutting board, cover with a tea towel; allow to cool. Peel, discard skin and cut flesh into thick strips. Place red pepper and remaining vegetables in large baking dish; coat with half the marinade. Bake for 15 minutes, turn and coat again with remaining marinade. Cook for another 15 minutes.

Cut the pasta into 24 sheets, each 10 x 16 cm (about 4 x 6^1/$_4$ inches). Make 6 individual stacks in the following order: pasta, courgette and sweet potato, 2 teaspoons pesto and bocconcini slices, pasta, aubergine and red pepper, pasta, tomatoes, 2 teaspoons pesto and bocconcini slices, pasta. Transfer the stacks to greased baking dish. Brush the tops with olive oil and sprinkle with grated parmesan cheese. Bake for 15–20 minutes or until heated through and tender.

EASY! 75 MINUTES SERVES 6

RICOTTA AND BASIL WITH TAGLIATELLE

250 g (9 oz) tagliatelle

10 g ($^1/_3$ oz) flat-leaf (Italian) parsley

25 g ($^3/_4$ oz) basil leaves

$^1/_2$ teaspoon olive oil

25 g (1 oz) chopped sun-dried capsicum (pepper)

125 g (4$^1/_2$ oz/$^1/_2$ cup) sour cream

125 g (4$^1/_2$ oz/$^1/_2$ cup) ricotta cheese

15 g ($^1/_2$ oz) freshly grated parmesan cheese

Tagliatelle is the pasta that comes in long flat ribbons. You can use fettucine as a substitute.

Cook the tagliatelle in a large saucepan of rapidly boiling salted water until *al dente*. Drain and return to the pan.

While the pasta is cooking, process the parsley and basil in a food processor or blender until just chopped.

Heat the oil in a frying pan. Add the sun-dried capsicum and fry for 2–3 minutes. Stir in the sour cream, ricotta and parmesan and stir over low heat for 4 minutes, or until heated through. Do not allow to boil.

Add the herbs and sauce to the pasta, toss to combine and serve.

REALLY EASY!   15 MINUTES   SERVES 2

RIGATONI WITH TOMATO, HALOUMI AND SPINACH

Cook the pasta in a large saucepan of rapidly boiling salted water until *al dente*. Drain, rinse under cold water and drain again. Allow to cool.

Combine the lemon juice and olive oil and season to taste. Toss the lemon dressing through the cooked, cold pasta and lightly toss through the tomato, haloumi cheese and spinach. Serve sprinkled with freshly cracked black pepper.

REALLY EASY! · 20 MINUTES · SERVES 2

100 g (3$^{1}/_{2}$ oz) rigatoni

- -

20 ml ($^{1}/_{2}$ fl oz) lemon juice

- -

60g (2$^{1}/_{4}$ oz) semi-dried (sunblush) tomatoes

- -

20 ml ($^{1}/_{2}$ fl oz) olive oil

- -

60 g (2$^{1}/_{4}$ oz) haloumi cheese, thinly sliced

- -

30 g (1 oz) baby English spinach

- -

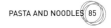

FETTUCINE
WITH GREEN OLIVES AND AUBERGINE

250 g (9 oz) fettucine
or tagliatelle

90 g (3¼ oz) green olives

½ large aubergine
(eggplant)

1 tablespoon olive oil

1 garlic clove, crushed

60 ml (2 fl oz/¼ cup)
lemon juice

1 tablespoon chopped
flat-leaf (Italian) parsley

25 g (1 oz/¼ cup) freshly
grated parmesan cheese
(optional)

Cook the pasta in a large saucepan of rapidly boiling salted water until *al dente*. Drain and return to the pan.

While the pasta is cooking, **slice** the olives and cut the aubergine into small cubes.

Heat the oil in a heavy-based frying pan. Add the garlic and stir for 30 seconds. Add the aubergine and cook over medium heat, stirring frequently, for 6 minutes, or until tender. Add the olives, lemon juice and season to taste. Add the sauce to the pasta and toss. Sprinkle with the parsley and grated parmesan.

REALLY EASY! 40 MINUTES SERVES 2 VEGAN

PENNE WITH ROCKET

Don't be tempted to use that 'no name' brand of pasta sauce with your weekly serving of penne! This simple and easy recipe really packs a sensational taste and more than justifies the short preparation time. One of my all-time favourites.

.Cook the penne in a large saucepan of rapidly boiling salted water until *al dente*. Drain and return to the pan. Place the pan over low heat. Add the butter, tossing it through until it melts and coats the pasta.

Meanwhile roughly **chop** the rocket and finely chop the tomatoes

Add the rocket to the pasta along with the tomato. Toss through to wilt the rocket. Stir in the pecorino cheese and season to taste. Serve sprinkled with the parmesan cheese.

100 g (3^1/$_2$ oz) rocket (arugula)

1^1/$_2$ tomatoes

250 g (9 oz) penne

50 g (1^3/$_4$ oz) butter

20 g (^{3}/$_4$ oz/^{1}/$_2$ cup) freshly grated pecorino cheese

freshly grated parmesan cheese, to serve

REALLY EASY!

12 MINUTES

SERVES **2**

POTATO GNOCCHI WITH TOMATO SAUCE

Tomato Sauce

500g (1 lb 2 oz) tomatoes, peeled and chopped

1 garlic clove , crushed

60 ml (2 fl oz) red wine

1 1/2 tablespoons finely chopped fresh basil

salt and freshly ground black pepper

300g (10 1/2 oz) ready made gnocchi

freshly grated parmesan cheese, extra, for serving

Any recipe which requires red wine gets my vote. Remember that you don't have to open a bottle of wine just to get the small amount you need for cooking — tempting as that may seem! To ensure that you always have some cooking wine to hand, freeze any party leftovers in an ice cube tray or plastic cup!

To make Tomato Sauce: In a pan, combine the tomatoes, garlic, wine, basil, salt and pepper. Bring to the boil. Reduce the heat and simmer gently for 20 minutes, stirring occasionally, until the sauce reduces and thickens slightly.

Cook the gnocchi in batches in a large pan of rapidly boiling water for 3–5 minutes each batch. The gnocchi will float on the surface when cooked. Drain well and keep warm while cooking the remaining gnocchi. Serve in warmed bowls, with the Tomato Sauce. Sprinkle with the extra grated parmesan cheese.

REALLY EASY!

15 MINUTES

SERVES 2

HOKKIEN NOODLES
WITH ASIAN GREENS AND GLAZED TOFU

Don't be put off by the need for kecap manis. Often referred to as Indonesian soy sauce, kecap manis is a syrupy, dark brown, soy sauce. It has a sweeter flavour than normal soy sauce and normally contains star anise, garlic and palm sugar for sweetness.

Cut the tofu into 1 cm (1/2 inch) thick slices and place in a shallow, non-metallic dish. Mix together the kecap manis, soy and oyster sauces and pour over the tofu. Leave to marinate for about 15 minutes, then drain and reserve the marinade.

Heat the oils in a wok over medium heat, add the garlic, ginger and onion and stir-fry until the onion is soft. Remove. Add the green vegetables to the wok and stir-fry until just wilted. Remove. Add the separated noodles and the reserved marinade and stir-fry until heated through. Remove from the wok and divide among four plates.

Fry the tofu in the extra oil until it is browned on both sides. Serve the noodles topped with the tofu, green vegetables and onion mixture.

REALLY EASY! | 40 MINUTES | SERVES 2

150 g (5 1/2 oz) firm tofu

30 ml (1 fl oz) kecap manis

1/2 tablespoon mushroom soy sauce

1/2 tablespoon vegetarian oyster sauce

1/2 teaspoon sesame oil

1/2 tablespoon peanut oil

1 garlic clove, crushed

1/2 tablespoon grated fresh ginger

1/2 onion, cut into wedges

225 g (1 small bunch) choy sum (Chinese flowering cabbage), roughly chopped

250 g (1 small bunch) baby bok choy (pak choi), roughly chopped

225 g (8 oz) fresh hokkien (egg) noodles, separated

1 tablespoons peanut oil, extra

SWEET GINGER AND CHILLI
VEGETABLES WITH RICE NOODLES

250 g (9 oz) fresh rice noodle sheets, at room temperature

1 tablespoon oil

$^1/_2$ teaspoon sesame oil

1$^1/_2$ tablespoons grated fresh ginger

$^1/_2$ onion, thinly sliced

$^1/_2$ red pepper (capsicum), sliced

50 g (1$^3/_4$ oz) fresh shiitake mushrooms, sliced

100 g (3$^1/_2$ oz) baby corn, halved

250 g (9 oz) Chinese broccoli (gai larn), sliced

100 g (3$^1/_2$ oz) snowpeas (mangetout)

1$^1/_2$ tablespoons sweet chilli sauce

1 tablespoon light soy sauce

1 tablespoon dark soy sauce

1 tablespoon lime juice

8 Thai basil leaves

Cut the noodle sheets into 3 cm (1$^1/_4$ inch) wide strips, then cut each strip into three. Gently separate the noodles (you may need to run a little cold water over them to do this).

Heat the oils in a wok, add the ginger and onion and stir-fry until the onion is soft. Add the vegetables and stir-fry until brightly coloured and just tender.

Add the noodles to the vegetables and stir-fry until the noodles start to soften. Stir in the combined sauces and lime juice and cook until heated through. Remove from the heat, toss through the basil leaves and serve.

REALLY EASY! · 35 MINUTES · SERVES 2 · VEGAN

PHAD THAI

This dish will certainly taste a lot better, and cost you far less, than a similar dish from that dodgy takeaway around the corner but you must serve it immediately after cooking. Sambal oelek is made from chillies and is available in jars from Asian supermarkets.

Cook the noodles in a saucepan of boiling water for 5–10 minutes, or until tender. Drain and set aside.

Heat a wok over high heat and add enough peanut oil to coat the bottom and side. When smoking, add the egg and swirl to form a thin omelette. Cook for 30 seconds, or until just set. Roll up, remove and thinly slice.

Heat the remaining oil in the wok. Cook the onion, garlic and pepper over high heat for 2–3 minutes, or until the onion has softened. Add the noodles, tossing well. Stir in the omelette, tofu, spring onion and half the coriander.

Pour in the combined soy sauce, lime juice, sugar and sambal oelek, then toss to coat the noodles. Sprinkle the bean shoots over the top and garnish with the peanuts and the remaining coriander. Serve immediately.

200 g (7 oz) flat rice-stick noodles

1 tablespoon peanut oil

1 egg, lightly beaten

1/2 onion, cut into thin wedges

1 garlic clove, crushed

1/2 small red pepper (capsicum), cut into thin strips

50 g (13/4 oz) fried tofu, cut into 5 mm (1/4 inch) wide strips

3 spring onions (scallions), thinly sliced on the diagonal

4 tablespoons chopped coriander (cilantro) leaves

30 ml (1 fl oz) soy sauce

1 tablespoon lime juice

1/2 tablespoon soft brown sugar

1 teaspoon sambal oelek

45 g (13/4 oz/1/2 cup) bean shoots

20 g (3/4 oz) chopped roasted unsalted peanuts

REALLY EASY! 35 MINUTES SERVES 2

UDON NOODLE STIR-FRY

3 spring onions (scallions)

250 g (9 oz) choy sum (Chinese flowering cabbage)

1 carrot

75 g (2³/₄ oz) snow peas (mangetout)

250 g (9 oz) fresh udon noodles

1 tablespoons Japanese soy sauce

1 tablespoons mirin

1 tablespoons kecap manis

¹/₂ tablespoon vegetable oil

1 garlic clove, crushed

¹/₂ tablespoon grated fresh ginger

50 g (1³/₄ oz) bean sprouts, trimmed

1 sheet roasted nori, cut into thin strips

Mirin is a sweet, low alcohol rice wine which adds sweetness and flavour to this dish. You can use ordinary rice wine instead if you wish. Roasted nori is edible seaweed and available from Asian supermarkets

Cut the spring onions and choy sum into 5 cm (2 inch) lengths. Cut the carrot into 5 cm (2 inch) batons. Cut the snow peas in half, diagonally. Add the noodles to a saucepan of boiling water and cook for 1–2 minutes, or until tender and separated. Drain and rinse under hot water. Combine the soy sauce, mirin and kecap manis in a small bowl.

Heat a wok with a lid over high heat, add the oil and swirl to coat the base and side. Add the spring onion, garlic and ginger. Stir-fry for 1–2 minutes, or until softened. Add the carrot, snow peas and 1 tablespoon water, toss well, cover with the lid and cook for 1–2 minutes, or until the vegetables are just tender. Add the noodles, bean sprouts and choy sum, then pour in the sauce. Toss until the choy sum is wilted and coated with the sauce. Stir in the nori just before serving.

REALLY EASY! — 25 MINUTES — SERVES 2

SWEET AND SOUR NOODLES AND VEGETABLES

I love pineapple and addig a tin to this dish is an in-expensive way of giving the recipe a sweetness boost!

Add the noodles to a large pan of boiling water and cook for 3 minutes; drain well. Slice the corn diagonally. Heat the oil in a wok; add the green and red peppers, celery, carrot and mushrooms. Stir over high heat for 5 minutes.

Add corn and noodles. Reduce heat to low; cook for 2 minutes. Blend cornflour with vinegar in a small bowl until smooth. Add chilli, tomato paste, stock cube, oil and undrained pineapple pieces to the bowl and stir to combine.

Pour pineapple mixture over ingredients in the wok. Stir over medium heat for 5 minutes or until the mixture boils and sauce thickens. Add the spring onion; serve immediately.

REALLY EASY! · 30 MINUTES · SERVES 2

100 g (3 1/2 oz) thin fresh egg noodles

2 fresh baby corn

30 ml (1 fl oz) oil

1/2 green pepper (capsicum), sliced

1/2 red pepper (capsicum), sliced

1 celery stick, sliced diagonally

1/2 carrot, sliced diagonally

125 g (4 1/2 oz) button mushrooms, sliced

1 1/2 teaspoons cornflour (cornstarch)

1 tablespoon brown vinegar

1/2 teaspoon chopped fresh chilli

1 teaspoon tomato paste

1 vegetable stock cube, crumbled

1/2 teaspoon sesame oil

225 g (7 oz) tinned pineapple pieces

1 large spring onion, (scallions) sliced diagonally

CHILLI SATAY NOODLES

250 g (9 oz) thin fresh egg noodles

1/2 tablespoon oil

1/2 teaspoon sesame oil

2 tablespoons peanuts, shelled, peeled

1 small red chilli, chopped and deseeded

2 slender aubergines (eggplants), sliced

100 g (3 1/2 oz) sugar snap peas

50 g (1 3/4 oz) bean sprouts

1 1/2 tablespoons crunchy peanut butter

1/2 tablespoon hoisin sauce

40 ml (1 1/4 fl oz/1/4 cup) coconut milk

1 tablespoon lime juice

1/2 tablespoon Thai sweet chilli sauce

Hoisin sauce is a spicy, vegetable-based sauce which is normally red-brown in colour. Available from all Asian food speciality stores.

Add the noodles to a large pan of boiling water and cook for 3 minutes. Heat the oils in a wok or pan. Add the peanuts and toss over high heat for 1 minute or until golden. Add the chilli, aubergines and sugar snap peas and cook over high heat for 2 minutes. Reduce the heat to medium and add noodles and sprouts; toss for 1 minute or until combined.

Blend the peanut butter, hoisin sauce, coconut milk, lime juice and chilli sauce until almost smooth. Add to the noodles. Toss over medium heat until the noodles are coated and the sauce is heated.

REALLY EASY!

20 MINUTES

SERVES 2

VEGETARIAN RICE NOODLES

Golden Mountain sauce is available from Asian food speciality stores.

Soak the mushrooms in hot water for 20 minutes; drain and slice. Pour boiling water over the noodles and soak them for 1–4 minutes until soft; drain well.

Heat a wok or large heavy-based frying pan. Add the oil and when hot add the garlic, ginger and tofu; stir-fry for 1 minute. Add the carrot, beans, red pepper and mushrooms to wok; stir-fry for 2 minutes.

Add the sauces and sugar; toss well, cover and steam for 1 minute. Add the noodles, bean sprouts and cabbage; toss, cover and steam for 30 seconds.

Arrange the noodles on a serving platter, garnish with bean sprouts and serve with chilli sauce. Serve immediately.

REALLY EASY! | **30** MINUTES | SERVES **2**

4 dried Chinese mushrooms

125 g (4^1/$_2$ oz) dried rice vermicelli noodles

1 tablespoon oil

1 garlic clove, chopped

2 cm (^{3}/$_4$ inch) piece fresh ginger, grated

50 g (1^3/$_4$ oz) fried tofu, cut into 2.5 cm (1 inch) cubes

1 small carrot, peeled and cut into fine shreds

50 g (1^3/$_4$ oz) green beans, cut into 3 cm (1^1/$_4$ inch) lengths

1 small red pepper (capsicum), cut into fine strips

1 tablespoon Golden Mountain sauce

^{1}/$_2$ tablespoon fish sauce (optional)

1 teaspoon soft brown sugar

50 g (1^3/$_4$ oz) bean sprouts

35 g (1^1/$_4$ oz) finely shredded cabbage

25 g (1 oz) bean sprouts, extra, scraggly ends removed, to garnish

Thai sweet chilli sauce, for serving

CURRY-FLAVOURED NOODLES

125 g (4¹/₂ oz) thick fresh noodles

30 ml (1 fl oz) oil

1 garlic clove, sliced

¹/₂ onion, finely sliced

¹/₂ red pepper (capsicum), cut into long, thin strips

¹/₂ small cucumber, unpeeled, cut into thin 4 cm (1¹/₂ inch) strips

1 teaspoon mild curry powder

60 ml (2 fl oz) vegetable stock

¹/₂ tablespoon soy sauce

¹/₄ teaspoon sugar

1¹/₂ spring onions (scallions), sliced diagonally

Add the noodles to a large pan of boiling water and cook until just tender; drain. Heat the oil in a wok or pan. Add the garlic, onion and red pepper and stir over medium heat for 3 minutes. Add the cucumber and curry powder and stir over medium heat for another 3 minutes.

Add the combined stock, soy sauce and sugar, stir until the mixture boils. Add the noodles and spring onions, stir over low heat for 3 minutes or until ingredients are well combined and heated through.

REALLY EASY! · 35 MINUTES · SERVES 2

NOODLES
WITH VEGETABLES AND HERBS

Score a cross in the base of the tomato. Put in a heatproof bowl and cover with boiling water. Leave for 30 seconds, then transfer to cold water, drain and peel away the skin from the cross. Cut the tomato into wedges and remove the seeds. Slice the onion and celery. Cut the chilli in half, removed the seeds and cut into strips. Slice the carrot, diagonally.

Heat the butter and a little oil in a saucepan. Add the onion, chilli, celery and carrot and cook over medium heat for 5 minutes. Add the seasoning mix, tomato, tomato paste, wine, bay leaf and stock to the pan and bring to the boil. Reduce the heat to low and simmer, covered, for 15 minutes, stirring occasionally. Add the herbs to the sauce and stir until combined.

Cook the noodles in a large saucepan of boiling water until just tender, then drain. Toss with the sauce to serve.

REALLY EASY! · 25 MINUTES · SERVES 2

1 tomato

$^1/_2$ onion

$^1/_2$ celery stalk

$^1/_2$ small red chilli

$^1/_2$ carrot

----

15 g ($^1/_2$ oz) butter

$^1/_2$ tablespoon Taco seasoning mix

----

1 tablespoon tomato paste (concentrated purée)

----

60 ml (2 fl oz/$^1/_4$ cup) red wine

----

1 bay leaf

----

60 ml (2 fl oz/$^1/_4$ cup) vegetable stock

----

1 teaspoon chopped basil

----

1 teaspoon chopped flat-leaf (Italian)parsley

----

185 g (6$^1/_2$ oz) thin fresh rice noodles

NOODLES IN BLACK BEAN SAUCE

185 g (6^1/$_2$ oz) thin fresh egg noodles

^{1}/$_2$ tablespoon dried, salted black beans, well rinsed (use Asian variety)

1 large spring onion (scallion)

^{1}/$_2$ teaspoon olive oil

^{1}/$_2$ teaspoon sesame oil

^{1}/$_2$ tablespoon grated fresh ginger

2 garlic cloves, crushed

1 tablespoon hoisin sauce

^{1}/$_2$ tablespoon black bean sauce

^{1}/$_2$ tablespoon sugar

60 ml (1 fl oz) vegetable stock

115 g (4 oz) tinned sliced bamboo shoots, drained

Dried, salted black beans are available from Asian speciality food stores.

Add the noodles to a large saucepan of boiling water and cook until just tender. Drain.

Chop the black beans and cut the spring onion into long slices.

Heat the oils in a wok or frying pan. Add the ginger and garlic and stir over low heat for 2 minutes. Add the black beans and stir for 2 minutes.

Add the hoisin and black bean sauces, sugar and stock to the pan. Simmer for 5 minutes until slightly reduced and thickened. Add the bamboo shoots, spring onion and noodles. Stir until heated through and all the ingredients are well combined. Serve immediately.

REALLY EASY!

35 MINUTES

SERVES 2

TOFU, PEANUT AND NOODLE STIR-FRY

As mentioned before, kecap manis is an Indonesian sweet soy sauce but if you are unable to find it, use soy sauce sweetened with a little soft brown sugar.

Cut the pepper in half, remove the seeds and membrane and chop. Cut the tofu into 1.5 cm ($5/8$ inch) cubes. Chop the onion and cut the broccoli into small florets. Combine the tofu with the garlic, ginger and half the kecap manis in a small bowl. Put the peanut butter, 125 ml (4 fl oz/$1/2$ cup) water and remaining kecap manis in another bowl and mix.

Heat a wok over high heat, add the oil and swirl to coat the base and side. Drain the tofu and reserve the marinade. Cook the tofu in two batches in the hot oil until well browned. Remove from the wok.

Put the noodles in a large heatproof bowl. Cover with boiling water and leave for 1 minute. Drain and gently separate the noodles. Add the vegetables to the wok (add a little more oil if necessary) and stir-fry until just tender. Add the tofu, reserved marinade and noodles to the wok. Add the peanut butter mixture and toss until heated through.

REALLY EASY! · **15** MINUTES · SERVES **2**

1/2 red pepper (capsicum)

125 g (4 1/2 oz) firm tofu

1/2 onion

60 g (2 1/4 oz) broccoli

1 garlic clove, crushed

1/2 teaspoon grated fresh ginger

40 ml (1 1/4 fl oz) kecap manis

45 g (1 1/2 oz) peanut butter

1 tablespoon peanut or vegetable oil

250 g (9 oz) hokkien (egg) noodles

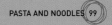

CHILLI SATAY NOODLES

2 slender aubergines (eggplants)

250 g (9 oz) thin fresh egg noodles

1/2 tablespoon oil

1/2 teaspoon sesame oil

25 g (1 oz) peanuts

1 small red chilli

100 g (3 1/2 oz) sugar snap peas

50 g (1 3/4 oz) bean sprouts, trimmed

30 g (1 oz) crunchy peanut butter

1/2 tablespoon hoisin sauce

40 ml (1 1/4 fl oz) coconut milk

1 tablespoon lime juice

1/2 tablespoon Thai sweet chilli sauce

The peanuts and peanut butter give this version of satay noodles a real crunch!

Slice the aubergine. Add the noodles to a large saucepan of boiling water and cook for 3 minutes. Drain, rinse well under cold running water and drain again. Heat the oils in a wok or frying pan. Add the peanuts and toss over high heat for 1 minute, or until golden. Add the chilli, aubergine and sugar snap peas and cook over high heat for 2 minutes. Reduce the heat to medium and add the noodles and the sprouts. Toss for 1 minute, or until combined.

Blend the peanut butter, hoisin sauce, coconut milk, lime juice and chilli sauce until almost smooth. Add to the noodles. Toss over medium heat until the noodles are coated and the sauce is heated.

REALLY EASY! 20 MINUTES SERVES 2

ORIENTAL MUSHROOMS WITH
HOKKEIN NOODLES

Once again, if you can't find, or afford, kecap manis use soy sauce sweetened with a little soft brown sugar instead.

Soak the hokkein noodles in boiling water for 2 minutes. Drain and set them aside.

Cut the red pepper in half, remove the seeds and membrane and slice. Slice the spring onions and shiitake mushrooms.

Heat the oils in a wok and swirl to coat the base and side. Add the garlic, ginger and spring onion. Stir-fry over high heat for 2 minutes. Add the red capsicum and the oyster and shiitake mushrooms and stir-fry over high heat for 3 minutes, or until the mushrooms are golden brown.

Stir in the drained noodles. Add the chives, cashews, kecap manis and soy sauce. Stir-fry for 3 minutes, or until the noodles are coated in the sauce.

REALLY EASY!

25 MINUTES

SERVES 2

125 g (4 oz) hokkein (egg) noodles

$1/2$ red pepper (capsicum)

3 spring onions (scallions)

100 g ($3^1/2$ oz) shiitake mushrooms

$1/2$ teaspoon sesame oil

$1/2$ tablespoon peanut oil

1 garlic clove, crushed

1 tablespoon grated fresh ginger

100 g ($3^1/2$ oz) oyster mushrooms

60 g ($2^1/4$ oz) snipped garlic chives

20 g ($3/4$ oz) cashew nuts

1 tablespoon kecap manis (see Note)

30 ml (1 fl oz) salt-reduced soy sauce

RICE,
GRAIN AND
PULSES

INTRODUCTION

Although there are literally hundreds of different types of rice, there are only two basic grains, long and short. Short rice is stirred during cooking to release the starch and produce a creamy, slightly sticky rice which is perfect for things like milk puddings, risottos or sushi. Long grain rice stays separate and should be washed well before cooking and not stirred whilst being cooked.

Pulses are the edible seeds of any legume, although the term usually refers only to the dried seeds. Pulses are an important protein source and staple food in many countries, especially in countries like India, where a large part of the population is vegetarian. In India, pulses are further split into 'gram', which are whole seeds and 'dal', split, skinned seeds.

Pulses do not keep indefinitely—they get harder as they get older and do not cook as well.

To quick-soak beans, put them in cold water with a pinch of bicarbonate of soda, then simmer for 5 minutes, leave to cool, then rinse and cook as for the recipe, or boil for 2–3 minutes, then soak in the same water for 1 hour.

Peas and lentils don't need to be soaked before they are cooked. Beans are usually soaked overnight to soften them but this is not strictly necessary—soaking may also start the germination or fermentation process if it gets too warm.

Kidney beans must be boiled for 15 minutes and then rinsed before cooking to get rid of the toxins on their skins. Soya beans must be properly cooked to inactivate their anti-nutrients and to make them digestible.

MUSHROOM RISOTTO

750 ml (26 fl oz/3 cups) vegetable stock

250 ml (9 fl oz/1 cup) white wine

1 tablespoon olive oil

30 g (1 oz) butter

$\frac{1}{2}$ leek, thinly sliced

250 g (9 oz) flat mushrooms, sliced

250 g (9 oz/1 cup) arborio rice

35 g (1$\frac{1}{4}$ oz/$\frac{1}{3}$ cup) grated parmesan cheese

1$\frac{1}{2}$ tablespoons chopped flat-leaf (Italian) parsley

balsamic vinegar, to serve

shaved parmesan cheese, to garnish

flat-leaf (Italian) parsley, to garnish

Place the stock and wine in a large saucepan, bring to the boil, then reduce the heat to low, cover and keep at a low simmer.

Heat the oil and butter in a large saucepan. Add the leek and cook over medium heat for 5 minutes, or until soft and golden. Add the mushrooms and cook for 5 minutes, or until tender. Stir in the arborio rice until it is translucent.

Add 125 ml (4 fl oz/$\frac{1}{2}$ cup) stock, stirring constantly over medium heat until the liquid is absorbed. Continue adding more stock, 125 ml (4 fl oz/$\frac{1}{2}$ cup) at a time, stirring constantly for 20–25 minutes, or until all the stock is absorbed and the rice is tender and creamy.

Stir in the parmesan and chopped parsley until all the cheese is melted. Serve drizzled with vinegar and top with Parmesan shavings and parsley.

EASY!   45 MINUTES   SERVES 2

RICE AND RED LENTIL PILAU

Basmati rice is predominantly used in Indian cooking. It has a light, dry texture and is lightly perfumed. The grains are very fluffy and stay separate when cooked, as well as elongating.

Heat the oil in a saucepan. Add the onion, garlic and garam masala. Cook over medium heat for 3 minutes, or until the onion is soft.

Stir in the rice and lentils and cook for 2 minutes. Add the stock and stir well. Slowly bring to the boil, then reduce the heat and simmer, covered, for 15–20 minutes, or until the rice is cooked and all the stock has been absorbed. Gently fluff the rice with a fork. Garnish with spring onion.

REALLY EASY! · 40 MINUTES · SERVES 2 · VEGAN

3 teaspoons garam masala

30 ml (1 oz) oil

$^1/_2$ onion, chopped

1 garlic clove, chopped

100 g (3$^1/_2$ oz/$^1/_2$ cup) basmati rice

125 g (4$^1/_2$ oz/$^1/_2$ cup) red lentils

375 ml (13 fl oz/1$^1/_2$ cups) hot vegetable stock

spring onions (scallions), sliced on the diagonal, to garnish

CRISPY LENTIL BALLS

125 g (4 1/2 oz/1/2 cup)
red lentils

2 spring onions
(scallions), chopped

1 garlic clove , crushed

1/2 teaspoon ground
cumin

40 g (1 1/2 oz) fresh
breadcrumbs

60 g (2 oz) grated
cheddar cheese

1/2 large courgette
(zucchini), grated

75 g (2 1/3 oz) polenta
(cornmeal)

oil, for deep-frying

I love to serve these lentil balls with chutney or yoghurt for dipping. Sensational!

Place the lentils in a medium pan and cover with water. Bring to the boil, reduce heat to low; cover and simmer for 10 minutes or until the lentils are tender. Drain and rinse well under cold water.

Combine half the lentils in a food processor or blender with the spring onions and garlic. Process for 10 seconds or until the mixture is pulpy. Transfer to a large bowl and add the remaining lentils, cumin, breadcrumbs, cheese and courgette. Stir until combined.

Using your hands, roll level tablespoons of mixture into balls and toss lightly in polenta.

Heat the oil in a heavy-based pan. Gently lower small batches of the balls into moderately hot oil. Cook for 1 minute or until golden brown and crisp. Carefully remove from the oil with tongs or a slotted spoon and drain on paper towels. Repeat the process with the remaining balls. Serve hot.

EASY! · **35** MINUTES · MAKES **15**

SWEET POTATO AND SAGE RISOTTO

Rinse the rice under the tap before using as this washes off any excess starch and helps the rice to remain separate when cooked.

Heat 3 tablespoons oil in a large saucepan and cook the onion over medium heat for 2–3 minutes, or until softened. Add the sweet potato and rice and stir until well coated in the oil.

Add 125 ml (4 fl oz/^{1}/2 cup) hot stock, stirring constantly over medium heat until the liquid is absorbed. Continue adding more stock, 125 ml at a time, stirring constantly for 20–25 minutes, or until all the stock is absorbed, the sweet potato is cooked and the rice is tender and creamy.

Add the parmesan and 1 tablespoon of the sage. Season well and stir to combine. Spoon into two bowls and drizzle with the remaining oil. Sprinkle the remaining sage over the top and garnish with shaved parmesan.

EASY! | 45 MINUTES | SERVES 2

25 ml (^{3}/4 fl oz) extra virgin olive oil

1 small red onion, cut into thin wedges

300 g (10^1/2 oz) orange sweet potato, peeled and cut into 2 cm (^{3}/4 inch) cubes

220 g (7^3/4 oz/1 cup) arborio rice

600 ml (21 fl oz/2^1/2 cups) hot vegetable stock

35 g (1^1/4 oz/^{1}/3 cup) shredded parmesan cheese

1^1/2 tablespoons shredded sage

shaved parmesan cheese, extra, to garnish

GRILLED POLENTA
WITH SHAVED FENNEL SALAD

170 ml (5^1/$_2$ fl oz/^{2}/$_3$ cup) milk

60 g (2^1/$_4$ oz) polenta

10 g (^{1}/$_4$ oz) parmesan

2 teaspoons butter

70 g (2^1/$_2$ oz) fennel

2 teaspoons lemon juice

1 tablespoon olive oil

1 tablespoon shaved parmesan

Polenta, also known as cornmeal. It is made from ground dried corn and is bright yellow in colour. Available in supermarkes and speciality stores.

In a heavy-based saucepan, **bring** the milk and 500 ml (17 fl oz/2 cups) water to the boil. Add the polenta, and whisk until thoroughly mixed. Reduce the heat as low as possible and simmer for 40 minutes, stirring occasionally to prevent it sticking. Remove from the heat, stir in the parmesan and butter and season well. Pour into a greased tray to set (it should be about 2 cm (^{3}/$_4$ inch) thick). When cold, cut into six wedges, brush with a little olive oil, and cook in a hot chargrill pan (griddle) or on a barbecue hotplate until crisp brown grill marks appear.

Slice the fennel as thinly as possible and chop the fronds. Toss in a bowl with the lemon juice, oil and half the shaved parmesan. Season with salt and black pepper.

Serve the chargrilled polenta with the fennel salad piled to one side, and the remaining shaved parmesan on top.

EASY! 65 MINUTES + SETTING TIME SERVES 2

CAULIFLOWER PILAF

Always cook your cauliflower in a non-aluminium saucepan because aluminium reacts with cauliflower and can turn it yellow.

Put the rice in a sieve and rinse under cold running water. Set aside to drain.

Heat the oil in a saucepan that has a tightly fitting lid. Cook the onion over medium heat, stirring frequently, for 5 minutes, or until soft and lightly golden. Add the spices and cook, stirring, for 1 minute.

Add the rice to the pan and stir to coat in the spices. Add the stock and cauliflower, stirring to combine.

Cover with the lid and bring to the boil. Reduce the heat to very low and cook for 15 minutes, or until the rice and cauliflower are tender and all the stock has been absorbed.

Fold the coriander through the rice, and serve immediately.

EASY! · 40 MINUTES · SERVES 2 · VEGAN

70g (2^1/$_2$ oz) basmati rice

3 teaspoons olive oil

1 small onion, thinly sliced

a pinch cardamon seeds

^{1}/$_4$ teaspoon ground turmeric

^{1}/$_2$ cinnamon stick

^{1}/$_2$ teaspoon cumin seeds

a pinch cayenne pepper

170 ml (5^1/$_2$ fl oz/^{2}/$_3$ cup) vegetable stock

270 g (9^1/$_2$ oz) head cauliflower

2 tablespoons chopped coriander (cilantro) leaves

FRAGRANT VEGETABLES
WITH COUSCOUS

1 tablespoon olive oil

1 small onion, chopped

1 garlic clove, crushed

$^1/_2$ tablespoon finely grated fresh ginger

1 teaspoon ground cumin

1 teaspoon ground coriander

$^1/_4$ teaspoon cayenne pepper

$^1/_4$ teaspoon Hungarian sweet paprika

200 g (7 oz) tinned chopped tomatoes

125 ml (4 fl oz/$^1/_2$ cup) vegetable stock

$^1/_2$ swede, peeled and cut into 3 cm (1$^1/_4$ inch) chunks

1 carrot, peeled, quartered and cut into 3 cm (1$^1/_4$ inch) lengths

200 g (7 oz) orange sweet potato, peeled and cut into 3 cm (1$^1/_4$ inch) chunks

1 courgette (zucchini), cut into 2 cm ($^3/_4$ inch) slices

135 g (4$^3/_4$ oz/$^3/_4$ cup) couscous

Don't be put off by the long cooking time for this recipe. The dish is simple to assemble and well worth the effort.

Heat $^1/_2$ tablespoon of the olive oil in a large heavy-based saucepan. Add the onion and cook over medium heat for 10 minutes, stirring occasionally, or until very soft and golden. Add the garlic, ginger, cumin, coriander, cayenne and paprika and cook, stirring, for 1 minute.

Add the tomatoes and stock, and stir, scraping the bottom of the pan. Add the swede and carrot, cover and bring to the boil. Reduce the heat to low and simmer, covered, for 15 minutes. Add the sweet potato and cook for a further 30 minutes, then add the courgette. Cook for 15–20 minutes, or until the vegetables are tender. Season to taste.

Put 250 ml (9 fl oz/1 cup) of water and the remaining olive oil into a saucepan, cover and bring to the boil. Add the couscous, turn off the heat and stand for 5 minutes. Uncover and fluff up the grains with a fork. To serve, divide the couscous between warmed serving bowls, and top with the vegetables and their liquid.

REALLY EASY! · **95** MINUTES · SERVES **2** · VEGAN

ONION AND PARMESAN PILAF

Melt butter in a large pan, add onion and garlic and stir over low heat for 5 minutes or until soft and golden. Add rice and stock, bring to the boil, stir once. Reduce heat to low; simmer, uncovered, for 5 minutes or until almost all the liquid has been absorbed.

Add peas, stir until combined. Cover pan, cook over very low heat for 10 minutes or until rice is tender. Stir in parmesan cheese and parsley, serve.

REALLY EASY!

25 MINUTES

SERVES 2

20g (^{3}/4 oz) butter

1 onion, chopped

1 garlic clove, crushed

150 g (5^1/2 oz) basmati rice

420 ml (1^2/3 cups) vegetable stock

80 g (^{1}/2 cup) shelled peas

2 tablespoons freshly grated parmesan cheese

2 tablespoons chopped fresh parsley

MUSHROOMS FILLED WITH SPICED QUINOA

100 g (3¹/₂ fl oz (/¹/₂ cup) quinoa

250 ml (9 fl oz/1 cup) vegetable stock

1 small bay leaf

1 small star anise

1 tablespoon oil

1 large onion, finely sliced

¹/₂ tablespoon ground cumin

¹/₂ teaspoon garam masala

75 g (2¹/₂ oz) feta cheese, chopped

¹/₂ tablespoon chopped fresh mint

1 teaspoon lemon juice

2 large field mushrooms

1 tablespoon olive oil, extra

Quinoa (pronounced keen-wah) is a grain grown high in the Peruvian Andes. It is favoured by vegetarians and is known as a 'super grain' because of its protein content. It is available from health food stores.

Rinse quinoa under cold water for 5 minutes or until water runs clear; drain. Place quinoa, vegetable stock, bay leaf and star anise into a heavy-based pan. Bring to boil, reduce heat and simmer for 15 minutes until quinoa is translucent. Remove from heat and allow to stand for 5 minutes. By this time the stock will be absorbed into the quinoa. Remove bay leaf and star anise.

Heat the oil in a large non-stick frying pan. Add onions and cook over medium heat for 10 minutes or until they begin to caramelise. Add the cumin, garam masala, feta cheese and quinoa. Cook for 3 minutes or until heated through. Remove from heat and stir in the mint and lemon juice.

Remove the stalks from the mushrooms, chop the stalks finely and add to quinoa mixture. Brush mushrooms lightly with extra oil, place fan-side down on a preheated chargrill or barbecue. Cook for 3 minutes or until browned (time will vary according to the size of the mushrooms); turn over and fill caps with the quinoa mixture. Cook for 5 minutes or until the mushrooms are tender. Serve hot with salad.

EASY! — 1 HOUR — SERVES 2

BROWN RICE AND **PUY LENTILS**
WITH PINE NUTS AND SPINACH

To get the best possible flavour, toast the pine nuts in a dry frying pan over medium heat, stirring constantly, until they are golden brown and fragrant.

Score a cross in the base of the tomato. Put in a heatproof bowl and cover with boiling water. Leave for 30 seconds, then transfer to cold water, drain and peel away the skin from the cross. Cut the tomato in half, scoop out the seeds and dice the flesh. Dice the onion, carrot and celery. Bring a large saucepan of water to the boil. Add 1 teaspoon salt and the rice, and cook for 20 minutes, or until tender. Drain and refresh under cold water.

Heat 2 tablespoons of the oil in a saucepan and add the onion, garlic, carrot and celery. Cook over low heat for 5 minutes, or until softened, then add the puy lentils and 125 ml (4 fl oz/$^{1}/_{2}$ cup) water. Bring to the boil and simmer for 15 minutes, or until tender. Drain well, but do not rinse. Combine with the rice, tomato, coriander and mint in a large bowl. Whisk the remaining oil with the vinegar and lemon juice and season well. Pour over the rice, add the pine nuts and English spinach, and toss to combine.

EASY! — 55 MINUTES — SERVES 2

1 tomato

$^{1}/_{2}$ red onion

1 small carrot

1 celery stalk

70 g (2$^{1}/_{2}$ oz) long-grain brown rice

30 ml (1 fl oz) extra virgin olive oil

1 garlic clove

70 g (2$^{1}/_{2}$ oz) puy lentils

1 tablespoon chopped coriander

1 tablespoon chopped mint

3 teaspoons balsamic vinegar

1 teaspoon lemon juice

1 tablespoon pine nuts

35 g (1$^{1}/_{4}$ oz/$^{3}/_{4}$ cup) baby English spinach leaves

VEGETABLE PILAF

Heat the oil in a large heavy-based pan. Add the onion and cook for 10 minutes over medium heat until golden brown. Add garlic and spices and cook for 1 minute until aromatic.

Add rice to pan and stir until well combined. Add vegetable stock, wine, tomatoes and mushrooms and bring to the boil. Reduce heat to low and cover pan with a tight-fitting lid. Simmer for 15 minutes.

Add courgette and broccoli to pan; replace lid and cook for another 5–7 minutes, until vegetables are just tender. Serve immediately.

EASY! | 30 MINUTES | SERVES 2 | VEGAN

60 ml (2 fl oz) olive oil

$1/2$ onion, sliced

1 garlic clove, crushed

1 teaspoon ground cumin

1 teaspoon paprika

$1/4$ teaspoon allspice

150 g ($5^1/2$ oz) long-grain rice

180 ml (6 fl oz) vegetable stock

70 ml ($2^1/4$ fl oz) white wine

1 large tomato, peeled and chopped

75 g ($2^1/2$ oz) button mushrooms, sliced

1 medium courgette (zucchini), sliced

75 g ($2^1/2$ oz) broccoli, cut into florets

CHICKPEA PATTIES
WITH CARAMELISED ONION

1/2 tablespoon olive oil

1 small red onion, finely chopped

1 garlic clove, crushed

1/2 tablespoon ground cumin

1 x 310 g (11 oz) tin chickpeas

15 g (1/2 oz) sunflower seeds

15 g (1/2 oz) finely chopped fresh coriander leaves

1 egg, lightly beaten

35 g (1 1/4 oz) besan flour

oil, for shallow-frying

caramelised onion

20 g (3/4 oz) butter

1 red onion, thinly sliced

1 1/2 teaspoons soft brown sugar

plain yoghurt, to serve

Besan flour is also known as chickpea flour.

Heat the oil in a frying pan, add the onion and cook over medium heat for 3 minutes, or until soft. Add the garlic and cumin and cook for 1 minute. Allow to cool slightly.

Blend the drained chickpeas, sunflower seeds, coriander, egg and onion mixture in a food processor until smooth. Fold in the besan flour and season. Divide the mixture into four portions and, using floured hands, form into patties. Heat 1 cm (1/2 inch) oil in a frying pan and cook the patties in two batches over medium heat for 2–3 minutes each side, or until firm. Drain on paper towels. Keep warm.

To **make** the caramelised onion, melt the butter in a small frying pan and cook the onion over medium heat for 10 minutes, stirring occasionally. Add the sugar and cook for 1 minute, or until caramelised. Spoon over the patties with a dollop of yoghurt.

EASY! · 50 MINUTES · SERVES 2

ALMOND SESAME SOYA BURGERS

Place the soya beans, almonds, onion, carrot and tamari into a food processor and process for 2 minutes or until roughly chopped. Transfer the mixture to a bowl; add oats, egg, chickpea flour, cumin, coriander and sesame seeds; stir to combine.

Shape mixture into 5 even-sized patties. Heat the oil in a large frying pan and cook the patties over medium heat for 5 minutes on each side, or until golden and heated through. Burgers are delicious served with a tangy plum and yoghurt sauce, or with a salad and maybe a toasted bun.

REALLY EASY! | **30 MINUTES** | **SERVES 2**

160 g (2¹/₂ cups) tinned soya beans

60 g (2¹/₄ oz) smoked almonds

¹/₂ onion, chopped

¹/₂ carrot, grated

¹/₂ tablespoon tamari

1¹/₂ tablespoons rolled oats

1 egg, lightly beaten

1¹/₂ tablespoons besan (chickpea) flour

¹/₂ teaspoon ground cumin

¹/₂ teaspoon ground coriander

1¹/₂ tablespoons sesame seeds

oil, for shallow-frying

 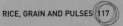

GREEN PILAU WITH CASHEWS

100 g (3^1/$_2$ oz) baby English spinach

50 g (1^3/$_4$ oz) cashew nuts, chopped

1 tablespoon olive oil

3 spring onions (scallions), chopped

150 g (5^1/$_2$ oz/^{3}/$_4$ cup) long-grain brown rice

1 garlic clove , finely chopped

^{1}/$_2$ teaspoon fennel seeds

1 tablespoon lemon juice

300 ml (10^1/$_2$ fl oz/1^1/$_4$ cups) vegetable stock

1^1/$_2$ tablespoons chopped fresh mint

1^1/$_2$ tablespoons chopped fresh flat-leaf (Italian) parsley

Make sure you don't overcook the cashew nuts. If you burn them they will taint the entire dish.

Preheat the oven to 180°C (350°F/Gas 4). Shred the English spinach leaves.

Place the cashew nuts on a baking tray and roast for 5–10 minutes, or until golden brown—watch carefully!

Heat the oil in a large frying pan and cook the spring onion over medium heat for 2 minutes, or until soft. Add the rice, garlic and fennel seeds and cook, stirring frequently, for 1–2 minutes, or until the rice is evenly coated. Increase the heat to high, add the lemon juice, stock and 1 teaspoon salt and bring to the boil. Reduce to low, cover and cook for 45 minutes without lifting the lid.

Remove from the heat and sprinkle with the spinach and herbs. Leave, covered, for 8 minutes, then fork the spinach and herbs through the rice. Season. Serve sprinkled with cashews.

EASY! | 1^1/$_2$ HOURS | SERVES 2 | VEGAN

FALAFEL

This dish tastes wonderful with a tahini yogurt dressing.

Put the dried chickpeas into a bowl and add enough cold water to cover them by about 12 cm (4½ inches) and leave to soak overnight.

Drain the chickpeas well and transfer to a food processor. Process until coarsely ground. Add the remaining garlic, herbs and spices and baking powder and process until smooth and a vibrant green colour. Leave to infuse for 30 minutes.

Using slightly wet hands, **shape** the falafel mixture into 12 ovals (about the size of an egg). Heat 5 cm (2 inches) vegetable oil in a wok or deep saucepan and fry the falafel in batches for 2–3 minutes, or until dark brown. Drain on paper towel and keep warm in a low oven while cooking the remaining mixture.

Arrange the rocket leaves on serving plates, top with the falafel. Serve immediately.

125 g (4½ oz) dried chickpeas

½ onion, finely chopped

1 garlic clove, crushed

2 handfuls parsley

2 handfuls coriander (cilantro) leaves

1 teaspoon ground coriander

½ teaspoon ground cumin

¼ teaspoon baking powder

vegetable oil, for frying

60 g (2¼ oz) rocket (arugula) leaves, to serve

REALLY EASY!

20 MINUTES + SOAKING TIME

SERVES 2

PEA AND ASPARAGUS SAFFRON RISOTTO

90 g (3¹/₄ oz/¹/₂ bunch) asparagus

pinch saffron threads

1 tablespoon olive oil

1 small onion, finely chopped

220 g (7³/₄ oz/1 cup) risotto rice

750 ml (26 fl oz/3 cups) vegetable stock

115 g (4 oz/³/₄ cups) frozen peas

15 g (¹/₂ oz) parmesan cheese, finely grated

Trim the woody ends from the asparagus, and cut the stalks into 3 cm (1¹/₄ inch) lengths. Add to the bowl, and cover with boiling water. Stand for 3 minutes, then drain and set aside until needed. Put 3 tablespoons of boiling water into a small bowl, and add the saffron threads. Set aside until required.

Heat the oil in a large, heavy-based saucepan. Add the onion and cook over medium heat for 5 minutes, until soft and transparent. Add the rice and cook, stirring, for 1 minute, until glassy. Meanwhile, put the stock into a smaller saucepan. Cover and bring to the boil, then reduce the heat to low and keep at a gentle simmer.

Add about 4 tablespoons of the hot stock to the rice, stirring constantly. When it has absorbed into the rice, add another 4 tablespoons of the hot stock. Keep adding stock, stirring between each addition, until the rice is tender and creamy. This will take about 25 minutes. Add the saffron and the liquid about halfway through adding the stock.

About 5 minutes before the rice is ready, **add** the peas and asparagus to the rice so that they will cook with the last addition of stock. Remove from the heat, and stir in the parmesan. Serve immediately, and top with freshly ground black pepper.

EASY! 50 MINUTES SERVES 2

SPICED BASMATI AND NUT RICE

Saffron is the most expensive spice in the world! Fortunately you only need a tiny amount of it when making this particular dish!

Soak the saffron threads in 3 tablespoons of boiling water until required. Put the rice in a sieve and wash under cold running water until the water runs clear.

Heat the oil in a saucepan, add the spices and fry gently over medium heat for 1–2 minutes, or until they start to release their aroma. Add the rice, nuts and raisins and stir well until all the grains are glossy. Add 250 ml (9 fl oz/1 cup) of cold water and the salt and bring to the boil. Cover and simmer gently over low heat for 15 minutes.

Remove the pan from the heat, remove the lid, and drizzle over the saffron water. Cover and leave to stand for a further 10 minutes. Stir through the coriander and serve.

REALLY EASY! · 40 MINUTES · SERVES 2 · VEGAN

small pinch saffron threads

125 g (4^1/$_2$ oz/^{1}/$_2$ cups) basmati rice

1 tablespoon vegetable oil

1 cinnamon stick

3 green cardamom pods, crushed

3 cloves

35 g (1^1/$_4$ oz/^{1}/$_4$ cup) blanched almonds, toasted

35 g (1^1/$_4$ oz/scant ^{1}/$_2$ cup) raisins

^{1}/$_2$ teaspoon salt

1 tablespoon chopped coriander (cilantro) leaves

TOFU BURGERS

2 teaspoons olive oil

$^1/_2$ red onion

70 g (2$^1/_2$ oz) Swiss brown mushrooms

115 g (14 oz) hard tofu

1 garlic clove

1 tablespoon chopped fresh basil

70 g (2$^1/_2$ oz) dry wholemeal breadcrumbs

1 egg lightly beaten

3 teaspoons balsamic vinegar

3 teaspoons sweet chilli sauce

50 g (1$^3/_4$ oz/$^1/_2$ cup) dry wholemeal breadcrumbs, extra

olive oil, for shallow-frying

2 wholemeal or wholegrain bread rolls

2 tablespoons mayonnaise

30 g (1 oz) semi-dried (sunblush) tomatoes

20 g ($^3/_4$ oz) rocket (arugula) leaves

sweet chilli sauce, to serve

Heat the oil in a frying pan and cook the onion over medium heat for 2–3 minutes, or until soft. Add the mushrooms and cook for a further 2 minutes. Cool slightly.

Blend 250 g (9 oz) of the tofu with the garlic and basil in a food processor until smooth. Transfer to a large bowl and stir in the onion mixture, breadcrumbs, egg, vinegar and sweet chilli sauce. Grate the remaining tofu and fold through the mixture, then refrigerate for 30 minutes. Divide the mixture into six and form into patties, pressing together well. Coat them in the extra breadcrumbs.

Heat 1 cm ($^1/_2$ inch) oil in a deep frying pan and cook the patties in two batches for 4–5 minutes each side, or until golden. Turn carefully to prevent them breaking up. Drain on crumpled paper towels and season with salt.

Halve the bread rolls and toast under a hot grill. Spread mayonnaise over both sides of each roll. Layer semi-dried tomatoes, a tofu patty and rocket leaves in each roll and drizzle with sweet chilli sauce.

EASY! · 55 MINUTES + CHILLING TIME · SERVES 2

TOFU WITH CARROT AND GINGER SAUCE

Drain the tofu, then slice each block into six lengthways. Place in a single layer in a flat non-metallic dish. Mix the juice, sugar, soy sauce, coriander, garlic and ginger in a jug, then pour over the tofu. Cover and refrigerate overnight, turning once.

Drain the tofu, reserving the marinade. Heat the oil in a large frying pan and cook the tofu in batches over high heat for 2–3 minutes each side, or until golden. Remove and keep warm. Bring the marinade to the boil in a saucepan, then reduce the heat and simmer for 1 minute. Remove from the heat and keep warm.

Heat a wok, add the bok choy and 1 tablespoon water and cook, covered, over medium heat for 2–3 minutes, or until tender. Remove and keep warm.

Put all the sauce ingredients in a saucepan, bring to the boil, then reduce the heat and simmer, covered, for 5–6 minutes, or until the carrot is tender. Transfer to a food processor and blend until smooth.

To **serve**, divide the bok choy among two plates. Top with some sauce, then the tofu and drizzle on a little of the marinade before serving.

REALLY EASY! · **55 MINUTES + MARINATING TIME** · **SERVES 2** · **VEGAN**

300 g (10$\frac{1}{2}$ oz) packet firm tofu

2 tablespoons freshly squeezed orange juice

1$\frac{1}{2}$ teaspoons soft brown sugar

1$\frac{1}{2}$ teaspoons soy sauce

1 tablespoon chopped fresh coriander (cilantro)

1 garlic clove

$\frac{1}{2}$ teaspoon grated fresh ginger

1 tablespoon oil

325 g (11$\frac{1}{2}$ oz) baby bok choy (pak choy)

100 g (3$\frac{1}{2}$ oz) carrots

1 teaspoon grated fresh ginger

60 ml (2 fl oz/$\frac{1}{4}$ cup) orange juice

2 tablespoons vegetable stock

MISO TOFU STICKS
WITH CUCUMBER AND WAKAME SALAD

1 1/2 cucumbers, thinly sliced

10 g (1/2 oz) dried wakame

250 g (9 oz) silken firm tofu, well drained

1 1/2 tablespoons shiro miso

1/2 tablespoon mirin

1/2 tablespoon sugar

1/2 tablespoon rice vinegar

1 small egg yolk

50 g (1 3/4 oz) bean sprouts, blanched

1 tablespoon sesame seeds, toasted

Dressing

1 1/2 tablespoons rice vinegar

dash soy sauce

3/4 tablespoon sugar

1/4 tablespoon mirin

Sprinkle the cucumber generously with salt and leave for 20 minutes, or until very soft, then rinse and drain.

To rehydrate the wakame, **place** it in a colander in the sink and leave it under cold running water for 10 minutes, then drain well.

Place the tofu in a colander, weigh down with a plate and leave to drain. Place the shiro miso, mirin, sugar, rice vinegar and 2 tablespoons water in a saucepan and stir over low heat for 1 minute, or until the sugar dissolves. Remove from the heat, then add the egg yolk and whisk until glossy. Cool slightly.

Cut the tofu into thick sticks and place on a non-stick baking tray. Brush the miso mixture over the tofu and cook under a hot grill for 6 minutes each side, or until light golden on both sides.

To **make** the dressing, place all the ingredients and 1/2 teaspoon salt in a bowl and whisk together well.

To **assemble**, place the cucumber in the centre of a plate, top with the sprouts and wakame, drizzle with the dressing, top with tofu and serve sprinkled with the sesame seeds.

EASY! · 45 MINUTES · SERVES 2

EGG FRIED RICE

Chop the spring onion. Beat the eggs with a pinch of salt and 1 teaspoon of the spring onion. Cook the peas in a saucepan of simmering water for 3–4 minutes for fresh or 1 minute for frozen.

Heat a wok over high heat, add the oil and swirl to coat the base and side. Heat until very hot. Reduce the heat, add the egg and lightly scramble. Add the rice before the egg is set too hard, increase the heat and stir to separate the rice grains and break the egg into small bits. Add the peas and the remaining spring onion and season with salt. Stir constantly for 1 minute.

REALLY EASY!

30 MINUTES

SERVES **2**

1 small spring onion (scallion)

2 eggs

25 g (1 oz) fresh or frozen peas (optional)

30 ml (1 fl oz) oil

225 g (8 oz/1 $^1/_2$ cups) cold cooked white long-grain rice (you will need 200 g/7 oz/1 cup of uncooked rice)

SILVERBEET PARCELS

70 ml (2¹/₄ fl oz) vegetable stock

2 teaspoons olive oil

¹/₂ onion

1 garlic clove

¹/₂ red pepper (capsicum)

85 g (3 oz) mushrooms

40 g (1¹/₂ oz) arborio rice

20 g (³/₄ oz) cheddar cheese

1 tablespoon shredded fresh basil

2 large silverbeet leaves

270 g (9¹/₂ oz) tinned chopped tomatoes

1¹/₂ teaspoons balsamic vinegar

¹/₄ teaspoon soft brown sugar

Heat the vegetable stock in a pan and maintain at simmering point. Heat the oil in a large pan, add the onion and garlic and cook until the onion has softened. Add the pepper, mushrooms and rice and stir until well combined. Gradually add 125 ml (4 fl oz/¹/₂ cup) hot stock, stirring until the liquid has been absorbed. Continue to add the stock, a little at a time, stirring constantly for 20–25 minutes, or until the rice is creamy and tender (you may not need all the stock, or you may need to add a little water if you run out). Remove from the heat, add the cheese and basil and season well.

Trim the stalks from the silverbeet and cook the leaves, a few at a time, in a large pan of boiling water for 30 seconds, or until wilted. Drain on a tea towel. Using a sharp knife, cut away any tough white veins from the centre of the leaves without cutting them in half. If necessary, overlap the two sides to make a flat surface. Place a portion of mushroom filling in the centre of each leaf, fold in the sides and roll up carefully. Tie with string.

Put the tomato, balsamic vinegar and sugar in a large, deep non-stick frying pan and stir to combine. Add the silverbeet parcels, cover and simmer for 10 minutes. Remove the string and serve with tomato sauce.

EASY!

1³/₄ HOURS

SERVES 2

BAKED POLENTA WITH THREE CHEESES

Remember that polenta is also known as cornmeal and is available from most supermarkets and delicatessens. Havarti is a Danish cheese with a full flavour.

To **make** the polenta, brush a 7-cup (1.75 litre/56 fl oz) loaf tin with oil. Put the stock and 500 ml (17 fl oz/2 cups) water in a large pan and bring to the boil. Add the polenta and stir for 10 minutes until very thick.

Remove from the heat and stir in the parmesan. Spread into the tin and smooth the surface. Refrigerate for 2 hours, then cut into about 30 thin slices. Preheat the oven to 180°C (350°F/Gas 4).

Brush a large ovenproof dish with oil. Place a layer of polenta slices on the base. Top with a layer of half the combined havarti, mascarpone and blue cheeses and half the butter. Add another layer of polenta and top with the remainder of the three cheeses and butter. Add a final layer of polenta and sprinkle the parmesan on top. Bake for 30 minutes, or until a golden crust forms. Serve immediately.

EASY! 65 MINUTES + CHILLING TIME SERVES 2

Polenta

300 ml (10 fl oz) vegetable stock

150 g (5 oz) polenta

30 g (1 oz) grated parmesan cheese

Cheese Filling

50 g (1¾ oz) havarti cheese, sliced

50 g (1¾ oz) mascarpone cheese

50 g (1¾ oz) blue cheese, crumbled

50 g (1¾ oz) butter, sliced thinly

30 g (1 oz) grated parmesan cheese

BARBECUE VEGETABLE AND
TOFU KEBABS

250 g (9 oz) firm tofu, cubed

$1/2$ red pepper (capsicum), cubed

1 courgette (zucchini), thickly sliced

2 small onions, cut into quarters

150 g ($5^1/2$ oz) button mushrooms,
cut into quarters

60 ml (2 fl oz/$1/4$ cup) tamari

60 ml (2 fl oz/$1/4$ cup) sesame oil

1.5 cm ($1/2$ inch) piece ginger,
peeled and grated

90 g ($3^1/4$ oz/$1/4$cup) honey

Peanut Sauce

$1/2$ tablespoon sesame oil

$1/2$ small onion, finely chopped

1 garlic clove , crushed

1 teaspoon chilli paste

125 g ($4^1/2$ oz/$1/2$cup) smooth
peanut butter

125 ml (4 fl oz/$1/2$ cup) coconut milk

$1/2$ tablespoon soft brown sugar

$1/2$ tablespoon tamari

$1/2$ tablespoon lemon juice

20 g/$3/4$ oz) peanuts, roasted and chopped

20 g ($3/4$ oz) sesame seeds, toasted

Soak 12 bamboo skewers in water for 2 hours. Thread the tofu, pepper, courgette, onions and mushrooms alternately onto the skewers. Lay out in a large flat dish.

Combine the tamari, oil, ginger and honey in a non-metallic bowl. Pour over the kebabs. Leave for 30 minutes. Cook on a hot barbecue or in a chargrill pan, basting and turning, for 10–15 minutes, or until tender. Remove and keep warm.

To **make** the peanut sauce, heat the oil in a large frying pan over medium heat and cook the onion, garlic and chilli paste for 1–2 minutes, or until the onion is soft. Reduce the heat, add the peanut butter, coconut milk, sugar, tamari and lemon juice and stir. Bring to the boil, then reduce the heat and simmer for 10 minutes, or until just thick. Stir in the peanuts. If the sauce is too thick, add water. Serve with the kebabs, sprinkled with sesame seeds.

REALLY EASY! | **70** MINUTES + MARINATING TIME | SERVES **2** | VEGAN

THAI TEMPEH

To **make** the Thai marinade, mix the lemongrass, lime leaves, chilli, garlic, sesame oil, lime juice, sugar and soy sauce in a non-metallic bowl. Add the tempeh. Cover and marinate overnight in the fridge, turning occasionally.

Drain the tempeh, reserving the marinade. Heat half the peanut oil in a frying pan over high heat. Cook the tempeh in batches, turning once, for 5 minutes, or until crispy, adding more oil when needed. Drain on paper towels. Heat the reserved marinade with the palm sugar in a saucepan until syrupy.

Put a slice of tempeh on each serving plate and top with some snow pea sprouts. Continue the layers, finishing with the tempeh on top. Drizzle with the reserved marinade and sprinkle with lime leaves.

REALLY EASY! · 35 MINUTES + MARINATING TIME · SERVES 2 · VEGAN

Thai Marinade

1 stem lemongrass, finely chopped

1 kaffir lime (makrut) leaf, shredded

1 small red chilli, seeded and finely chopped

1 garlic clove, crushed

1 teaspoon sesame oil

60 ml (2 fl oz/¼ cup) lime juice

1 teaspoons shaved palm sugar (jaggery)

60 ml (2 fl oz) soy sauce

300 g (10½ oz) tofu tempeh, cut into twelve 5 mm (¼ inch) slices

1½ tablespoons peanut oil

½ tablespoon shaved palm sugar

50 g (1¼ oz) snow pea sprouts or watercress

kaffir lime (makrut) leaves, finely shredded

ASPARAGUS AND PISTACHIO RISOTTO

500 ml (17 fl oz/2 cups) vegetable stock

125 ml (4 fl oz/^{1}/$_2$ cup) white wine

40 ml (1^1/$_4$ fl oz) extra virgin olive oil

^{1}/$_2$ red onion, finely chopped

220 g (7^3/$_4$ oz/1 cup) arborio rice

150 g (5^1/$_2$ oz) asparagus spears, trimmed and cut into 3 cm (1^1/$_4$ inch) pieces

60 ml (1^3/$_4$ oz/^{1}/$_4$ cup) cream

50 g (^{1}/$_2$ cup) grated parmesan cheese

20 g (^{3}/$_4$ oz/^{1}/$_4$ cup) shelled pistachio nuts, toasted and roughly chopped

Heat the stock and wine in a large saucepan, bring to the boil, then reduce the heat, cover and keep at a low simmer.

Heat the olive oil in another large saucepan. Add the onion and cook over medium heat for 3 minutes, or until soft. Add the rice and stir until the rice is translucent.

Add 125 ml (4 fl oz/^{1}/$_2$ cup) hot stock, stirring constantly over medium heat until the liquid is absorbed. Continue adding more stock, 125 ml (^{1}/$_2$ cup) at a time, stirring constantly for 20–25 minutes, or until all the stock is absorbed and the rice is tender and creamy. Add the asparagus during the last 5 minutes of cooking. Remove from the heat.

Stand for 2 minutes, then stir in the cream and parmesan, and season to taste with salt and black pepper. Serve sprinkled with pistachios.

EASY! 45 MINUTES SERVES 2

GRILLED POLENTA
WITH WILD MUSHROOMS

Just use button mushrooms if the other varieties aren't available.

Put the stock and 500 ml (17 fl oz/2 cups) water in a large pan and bring to the boil. Add the polenta and stir constantly for 10 minutes until very thick. Remove from the heat and stir in the parmesan. Brush a medium ovenproof dish with oil. Spread the polenta into the tin and smooth the surface. Refrigerate for 2 hours, turn out and cut into 6–8 wedges.

To **make** the sauce, wipe the mushrooms with a damp cloth and roughly chop the larger ones. Put the mushrooms, oil, parsley, garlic and onion in a pan. Stir, cover and leave to simmer for 50 minutes, or until cooked through. Uncover and cook for 10 minutes, or until there is very little liquid left. Set aside.

Brush one side of the polenta with olive oil and cook under a preheated grill for 5 minutes, or until the edges are browned. Turn over and brown. Reheat the mushroom sauce and serve spooned over slices of polenta.

EASY! · 65 MINUTES + CHILLING TIME · SERVES 2

300 ml (10^1/$_2$ fl oz/1^1/$_4$ cups) vegetable stock

150 g (5^1/$_2$ oz) polenta

50 g (1^3/$_4$ oz) parmesan, cheese grated

Mushroom Sauce

500g (1 lb 2 oz) mixed mushrooms (roman, oyster and flat)

^{1}/$_4$ cup (60 ml/2 fl oz) olive oil

^{1}/$_4$ cup (10 g/^{1}/$_4$ oz) chopped parsley

2 garlic cloves , finely chopped

^{1}/$_2$ onion, chopped

COUSCOUS PATTIES

90 g (3 oz) couscous

2 tablespoons oil

1/2 aubergine (eggplant), finely diced

1 small onion, finely chopped

1 garlic clove , crushed

1 teaspoon ground cumin

1 teaspoon ground coriander

1/2 red pepper (capsicum), finely diced

1 tablespoon chopped fresh coriander (cilantro)

1 teaspoon grated lemon zest

1 teaspoon lemon juice

2 1/2 tablespoons natural yoghurt

1/2 egg, lightly beaten

oil, for shallow-frying

Place the couscous in a bowl. Add 125 ml (8 fl oz/ 1/2 cup) of boiling water and leave for 10 minutes, or until all the water has been absorbed. Fluff up the grains with a fork.

Heat 2 tablespoons of the oil in a large frying pan and fry the aubergine until soft and golden, then place in a bowl. Heat 1 tablespoon of the oil in the pan. Add the onion, garlic, cumin and ground coriander. Cook over medium heat for 3–4 minutes, or until soft, then add to the bowl.

Heat the remaining oil and cook the pepper for 5 minutes, or until soft. Place in the bowl and stir well.

Add the vegetable mixture to the couscous with the fresh coriander, lemon rind, lemon zest, yoghurt and egg. Season to taste and mix well.

Using damp hands, **divide** the mixture into half and form into large patties—they should be about 2 cm (3/4 inch) thick. Cover and refrigerate for 15 minutes. Shallow-fry the patties over medium heat for 5 minutes on each side, or until golden. Drain the patties well and serve with yoghurt.

EASY!

65 MINUTES

SERVES 2

CARAWAY POLENTA WITH BRAISED LEEKS

Polenta is also known as cornmeal and is available from most supermarkets and delicatessens. Ready-made stock can be quite salty, so use half stock, half water.

Place the stock in a large heavy-based pan and bring to the boil. Pour in the polenta in a fine stream, stirring continuously. Add the caraway seeds and then reduce the heat and simmer for about 20–25 minutes, or until the polenta is very soft.

Melt the butter in a frying pan over medium heat and add the leeks. Cover and cook gently, stirring often, until wilted. Add the fontina, stir a couple of times and remove from the heat.

Pour the polenta onto plates in nest shapes and spoon the leeks and cheese into the centre.

750 ml (26 fl oz/3 cups) vegetable stock

110 g (3³/₄ oz/³/₄ cup) polenta

1 teaspoon caraway seeds

22 g (³/₄ oz) butter

1 large leek, cut into thin strips

125 g (4¹/₂ oz) fontina cheese, cubed

REALLY EASY! 40 MINUTES SERVES 2

CHICKPEA CURRY

1 onions

2 garlic cloves

$1/2$ tablespoon oil

$1/2$ teaspoon chilli powder

$1/2$ teaspoon salt

$1/2$ teaspoon turmeric

$1/2$ teaspoon paprika

$1/2$ tablespoon ground cumin

$1/2$ tablespoon ground coriander

1 x 440 g (14 oz) tin chickpeas, drained

220 g (7 oz) tinned chopped tomatoes

$1/2$ teaspoon garam masala

I love to serve this curry wrapped inside chapattis or naan bread. The perfect meal!

Slice the onion finely; crush the garlic. Heat oil in a medium pan. Add onion and garlic to pan; cook over medium heat, stirring, until soft.

Add the chilli powder, salt, turmeric, paprika, cumin and coriander. Stir over heat for 1 minute.

Add chickpeas and undrained tomatoes, stir until combined. Simmer, covered, over low heat for 20 minutes, stirring occasionally. Stir in garam masala. Simmer, covered, for another 10 minutes.

REALLY EASY! · 40 MINUTES · SERVES 2 · VEGAN

THREE-BEAN CHILLI

If you can't find black beans then double the quantity of kidney beans and chickpeas. Omit the sour cream for the vegan option.

Place the black beans in a large pan, cover with water and bring to the boil. Turn off the heat and set aside for 2 hours. Drain the beans, cover with fresh water and boil for 1 hour, until the beans are tender but not mushy. Drain well.

Heat the oil in a large pan and cook the onion over medium-low heat for 5 minutes, until golden, stirring frequently. Reduce the heat, add the garlic and spices; stir for 1 minute.

Add the tomatoes, stock, chickpeas, kidney beans and black beans and combine with the onion mixture. Bring to the boil, then simmer for 20 minutes, stirring occasionally.

Add the tomato paste, sugar and salt and pepper, to taste. Simmer for a further 5 minutes. Serve with sour cream and corn chips on the side.

REALLY EASY! | **2** HOURS + STANDING TIME | SERVES **2** | VEGAN

110 g (3 1/2 oz) dried black beans

1 tablespoon oil

1/2 large onion, finely chopped

1 garlic cloves, crushed

1 tablespoon ground cumin

1/2 tablespoon ground coriander

1/2 teaspoon ground cinnamon

1/2 teaspoon chilli powder

200 g (6 1/2 oz) tin chopped tomatoes

180 ml (6 fl oz) vegetable stock

200 g (6 1/2 oz) tin chickpeas, rinsed and drained

200 g (6 1/2 oz) tin red kidney beans, rinsed and drained

1 tablespoon tomato paste

1/2 tablespoon sugar

sour cream and corn chips, to serve

DHAL WITH VEGETABLES

50g (1^3/$_4$ oz) yellow lentils

50g (1^3/$_4$ oz) red lentils

2 teaspoons ghee

^{1}/$_2$ onion

1 garlic clove

1^1/$_2$ teaspoons fenugreek seeds

^{1}/$_2$ teaspoon ground cumin

^{1}/$_2$ teaspoon ground coriander

^{1}/$_8$ teaspoon ground turmeric

135 g (4^3/$_4$ oz) tinned chopped tomatoes

250 ml (9 fl oz/1 cup) vegetable stock

1 small carrot

85 g (3 oz) cauliflower florets

50 g (1^3/$_4$ oz) green beans

1 tablespoon cream

3 teaspoons chopped coriander

naan bread, to serve

Rinse the lentils, separately, under cold water until the water runs clear, then drain well. Put the yellow lentils in a small bowl, cover with water and stand for 30 minutes, then drain well.

Heat the ghee in a saucepan over medium heat. Cook the onion and garlic, stirring, for about 3 minutes, or until the onion is soft.

Stir in the spices and cook, stirring, for about 30 seconds, or until fragrant. Add the lentils, tomatoes and stock. Bring to the boil over high heat, then reduce the heat to low and simmer, covered, for 20 minutes.

Stir in the carrots and cauliflower. Cover and cook for 10 minutes. Add the beans and cook, covered, for a further 5 minutes, or until the lentils are tender and the vegetables are cooked. Season to taste. Stir in the cream. Serve the dhal sprinkled with the coriander leaves and serve with naan bread.

REALLY EASY!

1 HOUR + STANDING TIME

SERVES 2

BRAISED BUTTERBEANS
WITH LEEKS AND PEARS

Butterbeans (lima) beans originated in Peru and are named after the capital, Lima. They have a light buttery flavour and a creamy texture. Butter beans can be small or large: the smaller beans can be white or green, the large are only white.

Heat the oil in a large non-stick frying pan. Add the garlic, leeks and brown sugar and cook over medium heat for 10 minutes, or until the leek begins to caramelise.

Add the pear, tomato, fennel seeds, white wine and wine vinegar; simmer for 10 minutes or until the liquid has reduced by a quarter.

Stir in butterbeans, asparagus and sage; season with salt and pepper. Cook for 5 minutes or until the asparagus is tender. Sprinkle with toasted pine nuts and serve.

REALLY EASY! · 1 HOUR · SERVES 2

Note: To toast pine nuts, spread them on an oven tray and place in a preheated oven 180°C (350°F/Gas 4) for about 5 minutes or until golden.

1 tablespoon oil

1 garlic clove , crushed

1 leek, sliced

$1/2$ teaspoon soft brown sugar

1 pear, peeled and cut into thick slices

1 medium tomatoes, peeled, seeded and diced

$1/2$ teaspoon fennel seeds

125 ml (4 fl oz/$1/2$ cup) white wine

1 tablespoon white wine vinegar

400 g (14 oz) tin butterbeans, rinsed and drained

75 g (2$1/2$ oz) asparagus, cut into 4 cm (1$1/2$ inch) lengths

4 small sage leaves

salt and pepper

1 tablespoon pine nuts, toasted

FENNEL, TOMATO AND WHITE BEAN STEW

2¹/₂ tomatoes, peeled
seeded and chopped

1 leek, washed and sliced

1 garlic clove , finely chopped

¹/₂ large fennel bulb, washed,
halved, cored and sliced

1¹/₂ tablespoons extra
virgin olive oil

30 ml (1 fl oz) Pernod

1 fresh bay leaf

2¹/₂ sprigs fresh thyme

salt and freshly ground
black pepper

250 g (9 oz) desiree potatoes,
peeled and cut into large chunks

200 g (7 oz) tinned cannellini
beans, rinsed and drained

125 ml(4 fl oz/¹/₂ cup)
vegetable stock

125 ml(4 fl oz/¹/₂ cup) white wine

60 g (2¹/₄ oz) ready-made pesto,
for serving

The Pernod really adds flavour to this dish but there is no need to include it unless you have a bottle readily to hand.

Preheat the oven to moderate 180°C (350°F/ Gas 4). In a medium ovenproof dish combine the tomatoes, leek, garlic, fennel, olive oil, Pernod, bay leaf, thyme and black pepper. Mix well. (This should preferably be done well ahead of time to allow the flavours to develop.)

Cover the dish and bake for 30 minutes. Remove from the oven; add the potatoes, beans, stock and wine. Mix well and cover. Bake for another 35–45 minutes or until the potatoes are cooked through. Remove the bay leaves and thyme and discard them. Serve in warmed bowls, with a spoonful of pesto.

REALLY EASY! · 1³/₄ HOURS · SERVES 2

INDONESIAN COCONUT AND SPICE RICE

Basmati or jasmine rice can be used instead of long-grain rice, if you prefer. Avoid lifting the lid of the wok while the rice is cooking, as all the steam will escape, resulting in thick, starchy rice.

Cut the spring onion into 2.5 mm (¹/8 inch) slices. Heat the oil in a wok. Add the peanuts and cook, stirring often, until they turn golden brown. Add the coconut and stir until it darkens slightly and becomes fragrant.

Pour the coconut milk and 500 ml (17 fl oz/2 cups) water into the wok. Add the lemongrass stem, curry leaves and spring onion then bring to the boil. Reduce the heat and simmer for 2 minutes. Add the cumin, cardamom and turmeric, and bring to the boil again. Lift out the lemongrass stem, then add the rice and cook until steam holes appear at the surface of the rice.

Cover the wok with a tight-fitting lid, reduce the heat to very low and cook for 10 minutes. Lift the lid, check if the rice is cooked, and continue cooking (with the lid on) if required.

REALLY EASY! · **35** MINUTES · SERVES **2**

1 spring onion (scallion)

¹/2 tablespoon oil

40 g (1¹/2 oz/¹/2 cup) peanuts, roughly chopped

¹/2 tablespoon shredded coconut

125 ml (4¹/2 fl oz/¹/2 cup) coconut milk

5 cm (2 inch) lemongrass stem, white part only, lightly crushed with the side of a knife

4 curry leaves

¹/2 teaspoon ground cumin

¹/4 teaspoon ground cardamom

¹/4 teaspoon ground turmeric

250 g (9 oz/1¹/4 cups) long-grain rice

CASSEROLES, CURRIES AND BAKES

INTRODUCTION

The wonderful thing about these dishes is that their taste improves with age, so many of the recipes are perfect for keeping, reheating or even freezing. There is often less washing up to be done with these dishes too which is a big bonus for any time-starved student.

You can also consider preparing many of these recipes in advance. Do the cutting, chopping and peeling the night before you intend to cook but ensure you store the ingredients correctly.

The heart of any curry is the curry paste. The paste will infuse the other ingredients with its flavour and fragrance. Traditionally curry pastes are made by hand, the ingredients added one-by-one to a mortar for grinding or to the frying pan for roasting with the cook observing, smelling and adjusting as necessary. But today many of the prepared spice mixtures are just as good, although it is worth experimenting to find one that suits your particular tastes.

CELERIAC AND CARROT DAHL WITH NAAN

1 tablespoon olive oil

1/2 teaspoon yellow mustard seeds

1/2 onion chopped

1 garlic clove, crushed

1/2 tablespoon fresh ginger, finely grated

1 teaspoon cumin seeds

1/2 tablespoon ground coriander

1/4 teaspoon ground turmeric

1 teaspoon sambal oelek

180 g (6 1/2 oz/3/4 cup) black lentils, rinsed

1 small celeriac, peeled and cut into 2 cm (3/4 inch) chunks

1 carrot, peeled and cut into 2 cm (3/4 inch) chunks

1 handful mint, coarsely chopped if large

naan to serve

Black lentils are often available from health food shops and speciality food stores as Beluga lentils. If unavailable, use puy lentils instead.

Heat the olive oil in a large non-aluminium saucepan over low heat and add the mustard seeds. When they start to pop, add the onion, garlic and ginger. Fry for 5 minutes, stirring often. Add the cumin seeds, ground coriander, turmeric and sambal oelek, increase the heat and fry for 1 minute.

Add the lentils, celeriac and carrot and stir to coat. Add 750ml (26 fl oz/3 cups) hot water and bring to the boil. Reduce the heat and simmer for 10 minutes, stirring once or twice. Add more hot water if needed to just cover the lentil mixture. Simmer for 15–20 minutes, or until the vegetables are tender and most of the liquid has been absorbed. Season with salt, to taste, stir through the mint and serve with naan.

REALLY EASY! · 45 MINUTES · SERVES 2 · VEGAN

Note: To ensure a firm, uniform flesh, choose celeriac that are about the size of a grapefruit. those with smoother surfaces will be easier to peel. Once peeled and exposed to air, the flesh will discolour, so have a bowl of acidulated water on hand if the cut pieces are not to be used immediately.

CHOKOS WITH CASHEWS AND COCONUT MILK

Chokos (chayotes) are native to tropical America, and were eaten by the Aztec and Mayan peoples. Here, their delicate flavour is spiced up by the addition of ingredients common to the cooking of southern India — coconut milk, curry leaves and cashews.

Soak the cashews in water overnight. Drain and dry on paper towels. Finely chop half of the cashews by hand or in a food processor and reserve. Heat the oil in a saucepan and add the whole cashews. Fry over medium–low heat until golden. Remove with a slotted spoon and reserve.

Add the onion and garlic to the pan and fry until softened, about 5 minutes, then add the turmeric, cinnamon stick and curry leaves. Cook, stirring often, for 2 minutes. Add the coconut milk and 170 ml (^{2}/$_3$ cup) water. Bring slowly to the boil then simmer for 5 minutes.

Peel the chokos and cut each into 4 wedges. Discard the seed and slice the flesh into chunks. Add to the pan and return the mixture to a simmer. Stir through the chopped cashews and basil, remove from the heat and allow to rest for 2–3 minutes before serving. Serve with steamed rice.

75 g (2³/₄ oz/¹/₂ cup) raw cashew nuts

1 tablespoon vegetable oil

¹/₂ onion, finely sliced

1 garlic clove, crushed

¹/₂ teaspoon ground turmeric

¹/₂ stick cinnamon

4 curry leaves

200 ml (7 fl oz) coconut milk

2 small chokos (chayotes)

1 small handful Thai basil

steamed white rice to serve

REALLY EASY! 40+ MINUTES SERVES 2 VEGAN

THAI RED SQUASH CURRY

1 tablespoon oil

1 tablespoon Thai vegetarian red curry paste

200 ml (7 fl oz) coconut milk

1 tablespoon soy sauce

60 ml (2 fl oz/¼ cup) light vegetable stock

1 teaspoon grated palm sugar (jaggery)

350 g (10 oz) baby (pattypan) squash, halved, or quartered if large

50 g (1¾ oz) baby corn, halved lengthways

50 g (1¾ oz) snow peas (mangetout), topped and tailed

1 teaspoon lime juice

15 g (½ oz) unsalted roasted cashews, coarsely chopped

lime wedges to serve (optional)

If baby squash are unavailable, use courgettes (zucchini), cut into slices 2.5 cm (1 inch) thick.

Heat the oil in a large saucepan over medium–high heat and fry the curry paste for 1–2 minutes, or until the paste separates. Add the coconut milk, soy sauce, stock and palm sugar and stir until the sugar has melted. Bring to the boil.

Add the squash to the pan and return to the boil. Add the baby corn and simmer, covered, for 12–15 minutes, or until the squash is just tender. Add the snowpeas and lime juice and simmer, uncovered, for 1 minute. Serve with cashews scattered over the top, and accompanied by the lime wedges if desired.

REALLY EASY! | **35** MINUTES | SERVES **2** | VEGAN

Note: Thai cooking uses several kinds of curry pastes, each with a distinct flavour and colour obtained from its blend of herbs and spices. Red curry paste is highly fragrant, the commercial brands vary from medium to hot in intensity, so add more or less to suit your taste.

TAGINE OF FENNEL,
RED ONION AND DUTCH CARROTS WITH COUSCOUS

In North Africa, and particularly in Morocco, a tagine is an earthenware dish with a conical lid in which stews are simmered. The stews, also called tagines, are characterised by having both savoury and sweet flavours. They are served with couscous, as here, or rice. For a vegan option replace the butter with a suitable cooking oil.

Trim the tops off the fennel, leaving 2–3 cm ($^3/_4$–$1^1/_4$ inches) of stalks remaining, and discard the tough outer leaves. Halve the fennel lengthways. Peel the onions, leaving the ends intact. Trim the carrots, leaving 1–2 cm ($^1/_2$–$^3/_4$ inch) of stalks remaining. Scrub the carrots.

Put the stock in a flameproof casserole dish and add the fennel, onions, carrots, ground ginger, cumin, cinnamon, honey, garlic and cinnamon stick. Bring to the boil, then add the currants. Cover and simmer over low heat for 20–25 minutes, or until the vegetables are soft. Toss the mint leaves through the tagine.

Meanwhile, to **make** the saffron couscous, soak the saffron in 2 tablespoons hot water for 10 minutes. Bring the stock to the boil in a medium saucepan. Stir in the couscous and saffron with its soaking liquid. Cover and cook for 3 minutes. Remove from the heat and set aside for 5 minutes. Add the butter and toss with a fork to loosen the grains. Serve with the vegetables.

2 baby fennel bulbs

3 small (about 80 g/ $2^3/_4$ oz each) red onions

4 Dutch or baby carrots

180 ml (6 fl oz/$^3/_4$ cups) vegetable stock

$^1/_2$ teaspoon ground ginger

pinch ground cumin

pinch ground cinnamon

$^3/_4$ tablespoon honey

2 garlic cloves

$^1/_2$ cinnamon stick

1 tablespoon currants

$^1/_2$ handful mint

Saffron Couscous

small pinch saffron threads

310 ml ($10^3/_4$ fl oz/$1^1/_4$ cups) vegetable stock or water

180 g ($6^1/_2$ oz/1 cup) instant couscous

25 g (1 oz) butter

REALLY EASY!

35 MINUTES

SERVES **2**

VEGAN

CORN SPOONBREAD

125 g (4 1/2 oz/1/2 cup)
crème fraîche

1/2 egg

15 g (1/2 oz) grated
Parmesan cheese

15 g (1/2 oz)
self-raising flour

2 sweet corn cobs

a pinch of cayenne pepper

salt and freshly
ground black pepper

1 tablespoon grated
parmesan cheese

20 g (3/4 oz) butter.

Preheat the oven to 190°C (375°F/Gas 5). Combine crème fraîche, egg, parmesan cheese and self-raising flour in a large bowl.

Slice the kernels off 2 sweet corn cobs and add to the bowl. Add a pinch of cayenne pepper and salt and freshly ground black pepper, to taste.

Spoon into a greased small, shallow ovenproof dish. Sprinkle with 1 tablespoon grated parmesan cheese and dot with butter.

Bake in oven for 30–35 minutes, or until set and golden brown. Serve immediately, straight from the dish.

REALLY EASY! · 45 MINUTES · SERVES 2

BEAN AND PEPPER STEW

A delicious stew that is a real winter-warmer. It's flavours seem to come together after time, so it will taste even better the day after you cooked it. Keep a portion in the fridge in an air-tight container and you will have a ready meal for those days when your studies are so pressing that you don't have a minute to spare.

Heat the oil in a saucepan. Cook the garlic and onion over medium heat for 2–3 minutes, or until the onion is soft. Add the red and green capsicums and cook for a further 5 minutes.

Stir in the tomato, tomato paste, stock and beans. Simmer, covered, for 20 minutes. Stir in the basil, olives and sugar. Season well with salt and pepper before serving.

REALLY EASY! · 45 MINUTES · SERVES 2 · VEGAN

400g (14 oz) tinned haricot beans, drained and rinsed

1 tablespoon olive oil

1 large garlic clove, crushed

$^1/_2$ red onion, cut into thin wedges

$^1/_2$ red pepper (capsicum), cut into 1.5 cm ($^5/_8$ inch) cubes

$^1/_2$ green pepper (capsicum), cut into 1.5 cm ($^5/_8$ inch) cubes

1 x 400 g (14 oz) tin chopped tomatoes

1 tablespoon tomato paste (purée)

250 ml (1 cups) vegetable stock

1 tablespoon chopped basil

60 g ($^1/_3$ cup) Kalamata olives, pitted

1 teaspoon soft brown sugar

GREEN CURRY
WITH SWEET POTATO AND AUBERGINE

1/2 tablespoon oil

1/2 onion, chopped

1 tablespoon vegetarian green curry paste

1 small aubergine (eggplant), quartered and sliced

200 ml (7 fl oz) tin coconut milk

125 ml (4 fl oz/1/2 cup) vegetable stock

3 makrut (kaffir) lime leaves

1 small orange sweet potato, cut into cubes

1 teaspoon soft brown sugar

1 tablespoon lime juice

1 teaspoon lime zest

coriander (cilantro) leaves, to garnish

Some green curry pastes contain shrimp paste so if you want this dish to be truly vegan or vegetarian make sure that you avoid using any of those.

Heat the oil in a large wok or frying pan. Add the onion and curry paste and cook, stirring, over medium heat for 3 minutes. Add the aubergine and cook for a further 4–5 minutes, or until softened. Pour in the coconut milk and stock, bring to the boil, then reduce the heat and simmer for 5 minutes. Add the lime leaves and sweet potato and cook, stirring occasionally, for 10 minutes, or until the vegetables are very tender.

Mix in the sugar, lime juice and lime zest until well combined with the vegetables. Season to taste with salt. Garnish with fresh coriander leaves and serve with steamed rice.

REALLY EASY!   45 MINUTES   SERVES 2   VEGAN

COURGETTE PASTA BAKE

This dish has such simple flavours that it is important to use good-quality fresh ricotta from the delicatessen or the deli section of your local supermarket.

Preheat the oven to 180°C (350°F/ Gas 4). Cook the pasta in a large saucepan of rapidly boiling water until *al dente*. Drain well.

Meanwhile, **heat** the butter in a frying pan, add the spring onion and cook for 1 minute, then add the courgettes and cook for a further 4 minutes, or until soft. Cool slightly.

Combine the eggs, cream, ricotta, mozzarella, risoni and half of the parmesan, then stir in the courgette mixture. Season well. Spoon into two 500 ml (2 cup) greased ovenproof dishes, but not to the brim. Sprinkle with the remaining parmesan and cook for 25–30 minutes, or until firm and golden.

100 g (3$^{1}/_{2}$ oz) risoni

20 g ($^{3}/_{4}$oz) butter

2 spring onions (scallions), thinly sliced

200 g (7 oz) courgettes (zucchini), grated

2 eggs

60 ml (2 fl oz/$^{1}/_{4}$ cup) cream

50 g (1$^{3}/_{4}$ oz) ricotta cheese

50 g (1$^{3}/_{4}$ oz/$^{1}/_{3}$ cup) grated mozzarella cheese

35 g (1 oz/$^{1}/_{3}$ cup) grated Parmesan cheese

REALLY EASY! 50 MINUTES SERVES 2

SOYA BEAN MOUSSAKA

1 aubergine (eggplant)

$^1/_2$ tablespoon oil

1 small onion,
finely chopped

1 garlic clove, crushed

1 ripe tomato, peeled,
seeded and chopped

1 teaspoon tomato
paste (purée)

$^1/_4$ teaspoon dried
oregano

60 ml (2 fl oz/$^1/_4$ cup) dry
white wine

150 g (5$^1/_2$ oz) tin soya
beans, rinsed and
drained

1$^1/_2$ tablespoons chopped
flat-leaf (Italian) parsley

15 g ($^1/_2$ oz) butter

1 tablespoons plain
(all-purpose) flour

pinch ground nutmeg

155 ml (5 fl oz/$^3/_4$ cups)
milk

20 g (1$^1/_3$ oz) grated
cheddar cheese

Preheat the oven to 180°C (350°F/ Gas 4). Cut the aubergine in half lengthways. Spoon out the flesh, leaving a 1.5 cm ($^5/_8$ inch) border and place on a large baking tray, cut-side up. Use crumpled foil around the sides of the eggplant to support it.

Heat the oil in a frying pan. Cook the onion and garlic over medium heat for 3 minutes, or until soft.

Add the tomato, tomato paste, oregano and wine. Bring to the boil and cook for 3 minutes, or until the liquid is reduced and the tomato soft. Stir in the soya beans and parsley.

To **make** the sauce, melt the butter in a saucepan. Stir in the flour and cook over medium heat for 1 minute, or until pale and foamy. Remove from the heat and gradually stir in the nutmeg and milk. Return to the heat and stir constantly until the sauce boils and thickens. Pour one-third of the white sauce into the tomato mixture and stir well.

Spoon the mixture into the aubergine shells. Smooth the surface before spreading the remaining sauce evenly over the top and sprinkling with cheese. Bake for 50 minutes, or until cooked through. Serve hot.

EASY! 80 MINUTES SERVES 2

POTATO AND ZUCCHINI CASSEROLE

OK, so this does take nearly 90 minutes to cook but it is well worth the wait!

Preheat the oven to 180°C (350°F/ Gas 4). Remove the seeds and membrane from the red pepper and cut the flesh into squares.

Heat 2 tablespoons of the olive oil in a heavy-based frying pan over medium heat. Cook the onion, stirring frequently, for 10 minutes. Add the garlic and cook for another 2 minutes. Place all the other ingredients in a large bowl and season generously with salt and pepper. Add the softened onion and garlic and toss everything together. Transfer to a large baking dish and drizzle the remaining oil over the vegetables.

Cover and bake for 1–1½ hours, or until the vegetables are tender, stirring every 30 minutes. Check for doneness by inserting the point of a small knife into the potatoes. When the knife comes away easily, the potato is cooked.

REALLY EASY! — 1¾ HOURS — SERVES 2 — VEGAN

½ red pepper (capsicum)

30 ml (1 oz) olive oil

1 onion, sliced

1 garlic clove, crushed

200 g (7 oz) courgettes (zucchini), thickly sliced

200 g (7 oz) small waxy potatoes (pontiac, kipfler, desiree), unpeeled, cut into 1 cm (½ inch) slices

500g (1 lb 2 oz) ripe tomatoes, peeled and roughly chopped

½ teaspoon dried oregano

1 tablespoon chopped flat-leaf (Italian) parsley

1 tablespoon chopped dill

¼ teaspoon ground cinnamon

YELLOW CURRY
OF PUMPKIN WITH GREEN BEANS AND CASHEW NUTS

250 ml (1 cup) coconut cream (do not shake the can)

1$\frac{1}{2}$ teaspoon yellow curry paste

60 ml ($\frac{1}{4}$ cup) vegetable stock

250 g (9 oz) Jap pumpkin, peeled and diced

150 g (5$\frac{1}{4}$ oz) green beans, trimmed and cut in half

1 tablespoon soy sauce

1 tablespoon lime juice

$\frac{1}{2}$ tablespoon grated palm sugar

4 g (2 fl oz) coriander (cilantro) leaves

20 g (1 fl oz) cashew nuts, toasted

steamed jasmine rice, to serve

Spoon the thick coconut cream from the top of the tin into the wok, and heat until boiling. Add the curry paste, then reduce the heat and simmer, stirring, for 5 minutes, until the oil begins to separate.

Add the remaining coconut cream, stock and pumpkin, and simmer for 10 minutes. Add the green beans and cook for a further 8 minutes, or until the vegetables are tender.

Gently **stir** in the soy sauce, lime juice, and palm sugar. Garnish with the coriander leaves and cashew nuts and serve with steamed jasmine rice.

REALLY EASY!

45 MINUTES

SERVES **2**

VEGAN

QUICK MUSHROOMS
WITH RED CURRY SAUCE

It's worth pointing out here once again that not all curry paste is created equal. Make sure the curry paste you use does not contain shrimp paste for a truly vegetarian or vegan meal.

Place the coconut cream in a wok, bring to the boil and cook over high heat for 2–3 minutes. Add the curry paste and chopped lemon grass and cook, stirring continuously, for 3–4 minutes, or until fragrant.

Reduce the heat to medium, add the stock, coconut milk, soy sauce, palm sugar, lime leaves and lime juice. Cook, stirring, for 3–4 minutes, or until the sugar has dissolved. Stir in the assorted mushrooms and cook for 3–4 minutes, or until tender.

Remove from the heat, stir in the coriander and basil and serve with steamed rice.

REALLY EASY! · 35 MINUTES · SERVES 2 · VEGAN

250 ml (1 cup) coconut cream

1 teaspoon vegetarian red curry paste

1 teaspoon finely chopped lemon grass, white part only

60 ml ($^1/_4$ cup) vegetable stock

125 ml ($^1/_2$ cup) coconut milk

1 teaspoon mushroom soy sauce

$^3/_4$ tablespoon shaved palm sugar

2 small fresh makrut (kaffir) lime leaves

$^1/_2$ tablespoon lime juice

200 g (7 oz) assorted mushrooms (shiitake, oyster, enoki, button)

1 tablespoon coriander (cilantro) leaves

1$^1/_2$ tablespoons torn Thai basil

INDIAN-STYLE SPINACH

1 tablespoon ghee
or vegetable oil

1 small onion,
thinly sliced

1 garlic clove,
finely chopped

1 teaspoon finely
grated fresh ginger

$1/2$ teaspoon brown
mustard seeds

$1/4$ teaspoon
ground cumin

pinch ground coriander

$1/2$ teaspoon
ground turmeric

$1/4$ teaspoon
garam masala

175 g (6 oz) English
spinach, trimmed

30 ml (1 fl oz) cream

$1/2$ tablespoon lemon juice

Heat a wok until very hot. Add the ghee and swirl it around to coat the wok. Stir-fry the onion over medium heat for 2 minutes to soften. Add the garlic, ginger, brown mustard seeds, cumin, coriander, turmeric and garam masala, and cook for 1 minute, or until fragrant.

Roughly **tear** the spinach leaves in half and add to the spice mixture. Cook for 1–2 minutes, or until wilted. Add the cream, simmer for 2 minutes, then add the lemon juice and season with salt and freshly ground black pepper. Serve hot.

REALLY EASY!   20 MINUTES   SERVES 2

PUMPKIN WITH CHILLI

Peel the pumpkin, and scoop out the seeds to give about 300 g (10^1/$_2$ oz) of flesh. Cut the flesh into 1.5 cm (^{5}/$_8$ inch) cubes.

Heat the oil in a large frying pan or wok over medium heat, add the garlic, ginger and chilli, and stir-fry for 1 minute. Keep moving the garlic and chilli around the pan to ensure they don't burn, as this will make them taste bitter. Add the pumpkin, lime zest, lime juice, light soy sauce, stock, soy sauce and palm sugar, then cover and cook for 10 minutes or until the pumpkin is tender.

Remove the lid and gently stir for 5 minutes, or until any remaining liquid has reduced. Gently stir in the chopped coriander and serve immediately.

REALLY EASY! | 31 MINUTES | SERVES 2 | VEGAN

400 g (14 oz) butternut pumpkin (squash)

1 tablespoon oil

1 garlic clove, crushed

^{1}/$_2$ teaspoon grated fresh ginger

1 bird's eye chilli, finely chopped

^{1}/$_2$ teaspoon finely grated lime zest

^{1}/$_2$ tablespoon lime juice

^{3}/$_4$ tablespoon light soy sauce

90 ml (3 fl oz/^{1}/$_3$ cup) vegetable stock

^{1}/$_2$ tablespoon soy sauce

^{1}/$_2$ teaspoon shaved palm sugar (jaggery)

15 g (^{1}/$_3$ cup) coriander (cilantro) leaves, chopped

SPICY CHICKPEA
AND VEGETABLE CASSEROLE

165 g (5³/₄ oz) dried chickpeas

1 tablespoon oil

1 small onion, chopped

1 garlic clove , crushed

1¹/₂ teaspoons ground cumin

¹/₄ teaspoon chilli powder

¹/₄ teaspoon allspice

215 g (7¹/₂ oz) tinned peeled tomatoes, chopped

185 ml (6 fl oz) vegetable stock

150 g (5¹/₂ oz) pumpkin, cut into large cubes

75 g (2¹/₂ oz) green beans, topped and tailed

100 g (3¹/₂ oz) button squash, quartered

1 tablespoon tomato paste

¹/₂ teaspoon dried oregano

A quick way to soak chickpeas is to place them in a large pan and cover with cold water. Bring to the boil; remove from heat and soak for two hours. If you are in a hurry, substitute tinned chickpeas. Drain and rinse thoroughly before use. This is a good recipe to freeze and have on hand for those days when you need to maximise your study time.

Place the chickpeas in a large bowl; cover with cold water and soak overnight; drain.

Heat the oil in a large pan; add the onion and garlic and stir-fry for 2 minutes or until tender. Add the cumin, chilli powder and allspice; stir-fry for 1 minute. Add the chickpeas, tomatoes and stock to the pan. Bring to the boil; reduce heat and simmer, covered, for 1 hour, stirring occasionally.

Add the pumpkin, beans, squash, tomato paste and oregano. Stir to combine. Simmer, covered, for another 15 minutes. Remove the lid from the pan and simmer, uncovered, for another 10 minutes to reduce and thicken sauce slightly.

REALLY EASY! | 2 HOURS | SERVES 2

CARROT PESTO BAKE

Brush a 30 x 20 cm (12 x 8 inch) ovenproof baking dish with melted butter or oil. Heat the butter in a large pan; add the flour. Stir over low heat until mixture is lightly golden and bubbling. Add combined milk, sour cream and pepper gradually to pan, stirring until mixture is smooth between each addition. Stir constantly over medium heat for 5 minutes, or until the mixture boils and thickens. Boil for another minute; remove from heat. Stir in cheese; cool slightly. Gradually add beaten eggs, stirring constantly.

Pour a third of the sauce into another bowl to make the topping and set aside. Add the pesto and grated carrot to the remaining sauce, stirring to combine.

Preheat the oven to 150°C (300°F/Gas 2). Beginning with one-third of the carrot mixture, alternate layers of carrot mixture with sheets of lasagne in prepared dish. Use three layers of each, finishing with lasagne sheets. Spread reserved sauce evenly over the top. Sprinkle with extra cheese. Set aside for 15 minutes before cooking to allow the pasta to soften. Bake for 40 minutes or until sauce has set and is golden.

Remove from the oven; cover and set aside for 15 minutes prior to serving—this will ensure that it will slice cleanly and more easily. Serve with a crisp green salad.

50 g (1³/₄ oz) butter

60 g (2¹/₄ oz) plain (all purpose) flour

750 ml (26 fl oz/ 3 cups) milk

160 g (5¹/₂ oz/²/₃ cup) light sour cream

1 teaspoon cracked black pepper

100 g (3¹/₃ oz) cheddar cheese, grated

4 eggs, lightly beaten

2 tablespoons ready-made pesto

750 g (1 lb 10 oz) carrots, peeled and grated

250 g (9 oz) instant lasagne sheets

50 g (1²/₃ oz) Cheddar cheese, grated, extra

REALLY EASY! 1³/₄ HOURS SERVES 2

HUNGARIAN CASSEROLE

2 large potatoes

1/2 tablespoon olive oil

15 g (1/2 oz) butter

1 small onion, chopped

1/2 red and 1/2 green pepper (capsicum), roughly chopped

220 g (7 3/4 oz) tin chopped tomatoes

125 ml (4 fl oz/1/2 cup) vegetable stock

1 teaspoon caraway seeds

1 teaspoon paprika

salt and freshly ground black pepper

Crispy Croutons

125 ml (4 fl oz/1/2 cup) oil

2 slices white bread, crusts removed and cut into small cubes

I love to make my own crispy croutons to serve with this dish but you can substitute any crusty bread if you wish. For a vegan meal omit the butter and double the amount of oil .

Peel the potatoes; cut into large chunks. Heat the oil and butter in a large heavy-based pan; cook the potatoes over medium heat, turning regularly, until crisp on the edges.

Add the onion and red and green peppers; cook for 5 minutes. Add tomatoes with juice, vegetable stock, caraway seeds and paprika. Season to taste with salt and pepper. Simmer, uncovered, for 10 minutes or until potatoes are tender. Serve with Crispy Croutons.

To make Croutons: Heat oil in a frying pan over medium heat. Cook croutons, turning often, for 2 minutes or until golden brown and crisp. Drain on kitchen paper.

REALLY EASY! — 1 HOUR — SERVES 2 — VEGAN

WINTER VEGETABLE CASSEROLE

1 medium potato

$^1/_2$ medium parsnip

100 g (3$^1/_2$ oz) pumpkin

15 g ($^1/_2$ oz) butter

$^1/_2$ tablespoon plain (all purpose) flour

185 ml (6 fl oz/$^3/_4$ cup) milk

$^1/_4$ teaspoon ground nutmeg

salt and freshly ground black pepper, to taste

Crumble Topping

40 g (1$^1/_2$ oz) fresh breadcrumbs

50 g (1$^3/_4$ oz) roasted cashew nuts, roughly chopped

15 g ($^1/_2$ oz) butter

This quickly became one of my signature dishes. You don't have to make your own breadcrumbs of course as any store-bought ones will suffice.

Peel potato, parsnip and pumpkin; cut the pumpkin into large bite-sized pieces and potato and parsnip into smaller pieces. Cook vegetables in a large pan of boiling water for 8 minutes or until just tender. Drain and then arrange cooked vegetables in base of a large, deep ovenproof dish.

Melt butter in a pan over low heat. Add flour and cook, stirring constantly, for 1 minute. Remove from the heat and gradually stir in milk. Return pan to heat, bring mixture to the boil, stirring constantly, until thickened; boil for another minute. Add the nutmeg and salt and pepper; pour sauce over the vegetables. Preheat the oven to 180°C (350°F/Gas 4).

To make Crumble Topping: Combine the breadcrumbs and cashews. Sprinkle them over the vegetables. Dot the crumble topping with butter; bake for 30 minutes or until golden. Garnish with cress, if desired.

REALLY EASY! · 65 MINUTES · SERVES 2

LAYERED POTATO AND APPLE BAKE

To prevent potatoes and apples browning before assembling dish, place in a bowl of cold water with a squeeze of lemon juice. Drain and pat dry with paper towels before using.

Preheat the oven to 180°C (350°F/Gas 4). Brush a large, shallow ovenproof dish with melted butter or oil. Peel the potatoes and cut into thin slices. Peel, core and quarter the apples. Cut into thin slices. Slice the peeled onion into very fine rings.

Layer the potato, apples and onion in the prepared dish, ending with a layer of potato. Sprinkle evenly with cheese. Pour the cream over the top, covering as evenly as possible.

Sprinkle with nutmeg and black pepper, to taste. Bake for 45 minutes or until golden brown. Remove from the oven and allow to stand for 5 minutes before serving.

1 large potato

2 small green apples

1 medium onion

30 g (1 oz) finely grated cheddar cheese

(125 ml (4 fl oz/^{1}/$_2$ cup) cream

pinch ground nutmeg

freshly ground black pepper

REALLY EASY!

1^1/$_4$ HOURS

SERVES 2

AUBERGINE AND TOMATO BAKE

1 aubergine (eggplant)

1 tablespoon olive oil

1 small onion

$1/2$ teaspoon ground cumin

80 ml ($2^1/2$ fl oz/$1/3$ cup) good-quality white wine

270 g ($9^1/2$ oz) tin tomatoes, crushed

1 garlic clove

1 red chilli

2 tablespoons currants

1 tablespoon chopped fresh coriander

Preheat the oven to 210°C (415°F/Gas 6–7). Cut the aubergines into 2 cm (3/4 inch) thick rounds. Place on a tray and sprinkle generously with salt. Set aside for 20 minutes.

Heat 2 tablespoons of oil in a large pan. Add the onion and cook over medium heat for 5 minutes or until softened. Add the cumin and stir for 1 minute. Add the wine. Bring to boil; reduce heat and simmer for 10 minutes, or until the mixture has reduced by three-quarters. Add the tomatoes. Bring to the boil; reduce the heat and cook for 10 minutes. Add the garlic, chillies and currants. Simmer for 5 minutes; remove from the heat. Rinse the aubergine slices and squeeze them dry using paper towels. Heat the remaining oil in a large frying pan. Fry the aubergine slices over medium heat for 3–4 minutes. Drain on paper towels.

Layer the aubergine slices and tomato mixture in a large ovenproof dish, sprinkle fresh coriander between each layer. Finish with a layer of aubergine. Bake for 30 minutes. Serve with pasta.

REALLY EASY! — 1½ HOURS — SERVES 2 — VEGAN

POTATO CURRY WITH SESAME SEEDS

Boil, steam or microwave the potatoes until tender. Cool, peel and chop. Heat the oil in a large heavy-based pan over medium heat. Cook the cumin, coriander and mustard seeds for 1 minute, stirring constantly.

Add the sesame seeds; cook for 1–2 minutes, stirring until golden. Add the turmeric, chillies, potatoes, lemon zest and juice. Stir until well combined and heated through. Season, to taste, with salt and pepper.

REALLY EASY! **40** MINUTES SERVES **2** VEGAN

2 large potatoes

$1/2$ tablespoon oil

$1/2$ teaspoon cumin seeds

$1/2$ teaspoon coriander seeds

1 teaspoon mustard seeds

1 tablespoon sesame seeds

$1/4$ teaspoon turmeric

$1/2$ teaspoon chopped fresh chilli

1 teaspoon finely grated lemon zest

1 tablespoon lemon juice

salt and pepper

VEGETABLE CURRY

¹/2 tablespoon brown
mustard seeds

1 tablespoon ghee or oil

1 onion, chopped

2 tablespoons mild
curry paste

200 g (7 oz)
tinned tomatoes

60 g (2¹/4 oz) plain
yoghurt

125 ml (4 fl oz/¹/2 cup)
coconut milk

1 carrot, sliced

110 g (3³/4 oz)
cauliflower florets

1 slender aubergine
(eggplant), sliced

110 g (3¹/2 oz) green
beans, halved

75 g (2¹/2 oz)
broccoli florets

1 zucchini
(courgette), sliced

45 g (1¹/2 oz) baby button
mushrooms

Add a pinch of sugar to the tin of tomatoes if you find they taste too acidic.

Place the mustard seeds in a dry pan and heat until they start to pop. Add the ghee or oil and onions to the pan; cook, stirring, until the onion are just soft. Add the curry paste and stir for 1 minute until the mixture is fragrant.

Add the tomatoes, yoghurt and coconut milk; stir over low heat until combined. Add the carrots and simmer, uncovered, for 5 minutes.

Add the cauliflower and aubergine; simmer for 5 minutes. Stir in the remaining ingredients; simmer, uncovered, for 10–12 minutes. Serve hot with steamed rice.

REALLY EASY!　35 MINUTES　SERVES 2

RATATOUILLE

As with any good ratatouille you can vary the vegetables you are using in order to make best use of what you have to hand.

Heat the oil in a large, heavy-based pan and cook the onions over medium heat for 4 minutes or until soft. Add the courgette, peppers and garlic, stir for 3 minutes.

Cut the aubergine in chunks and add to the pan with the tomatoes, basil or oregano and pepper; bring to boil. Reduce the heat to simmer and cook, covered, for 15–20 minutes or until the vegetables are tender. Garnish with parsley and serve with crusty bread.

REALLY EASY! 40 MINUTES SERVES 2 VEGAN

1 tablespoon olive oil

1 medium onion, cut in wedges

1 medium courgette (zucchini), cut in thick sticks

$1/2$ small red pepper (capsicum), cut in squares

$1/2$ small green pepper (capsicum), cut in squares

$1/2$ small yellow pepper (capsicum), cut in squares

1 garlic clove, crushed

$1/2$ medium aubergine (eggplant), halved

220 g ($7^3/4$ oz) tinned tomatoes, crushed

$1/4$ teaspoon dried basil or oregano leaves

freshly ground black pepper

fresh parsley sprigs (optional)

MUSHROOM NUT ROAST
WITH TOMATO SAUCE

2 tablespoons olive oil

1 large onion, diced

2 garlic cloves, crushed

300 g (10^1/$_2$ oz) cap mushrooms, finely chopped

200 g (7 oz) cashew nuts

200 g (7 oz) brazil nuts

125 g (4^1/$_2$ oz/1 cup) grated cheddar

30 g (1 oz) parmesan cheese, grated

1 egg, lightly beaten

2 tablespoons fresh chives

80 g (2^3/$_4$ oz/1 cup) fresh wholemeal breadcrumbs

Tomato Sauce

1^1/$_2$ tablespoons olive oil

1 onion, finely chopped

1 garlic clove, crushed

400 g (14 oz) tin tomatoes

1 tablespoon tomato paste

1 teaspoon caster sugar

This is another dish that you can make in large quantities and then freeze.

Preheat the oven to moderate 180°C (350°F/ Gas 4). Grease a 15 x 20 cm (6 x 8 inch) tin and line with baking paper. Heat the oil in a frying pan and fry the onion, garlic and mushrooms over medium heat for 2–3 minutes, or until soft. Cool.

Finely **chop** the nuts in a food processor, but do not overprocess.

Combine the nuts, mushroom mixture, cheeses, egg, chives and breadcrumbs in a bowl. Press into the tin and bake for 45 minutes until firm. Leave for 5 minutes, then turn out.

Meanwhile, to **make** the sauce, heat the oil in a frying pan and add the onion and garlic. Cook over low heat for 5 minutes, or until soft. Add the tin of chopped tomatoes, tomato paste, sugar and 80 ml (2^1/$_2$ fl oz/^{1}/$_3$ cup) water. Simmer for 3–5 minutes, or until thick. Season. Serve with the sliced roast.

REALLY EASY! · 1¼ HOURS · SERVES 2 · VEGAN

AUBERGINE PARMIGIANA

Another recipe that freezes really well. Simply allow the dish to cool and then place individual servings in freezer bags or airtight containers. Don't forget to name each bag so that you know exactly what it contains.

Heat the oil in a large frying pan; add the onion and cook over moderate heat until soft. Add the garlic and cook for 1 minute. Add the tomato and simmer for 15 minutes. Season with salt to taste. Preheat the oven to 200°C (400°F/Gas 6).

Slice the aubergines very thinly and shallow-fry in oil in batches for 3–4 minutes, or until golden brown. Drain on paper towels.

Place one-third of the aubergines in a 7-cup (1.75 litre) ovenproof dish. Top with half the bocconcini and cheddar. Repeat the layers, finishing with a layer of aubergine.

Pour the tomato mixture over the aubergine. Scatter with torn basil leaves, then parmesan. Bake for 40 minutes.

EASY! · 1¾ HOURS · SERVES 6

Variation: If you prefer not to fry the aubergine, brush it lightly with oil and brown lightly under a hot grill.

3 tablespoons olive oil

1 onion, diced

2 garlic cloves, crushed

1.25 kg (2 lb 12 oz) tomatoes, peeled and chopped

1 kg (2 lb) aubergine

250 g (9 oz) bocconcini, sliced

185 g (6½ oz) cheddar cheese, finely grated

2 large handfuls basil leaves

50 g (1¾ oz/½ cup) grated Parmesan

MUSHROOM MOUSSAKA

½ aubergine (125 g/ 4 oz), cut into 1 cm (½ inch) slices

½ large potato, cut into 1 cm (½ inch) slices

15 g (½ oz) butter

½ onion, finely chopped

1 garlic clove , finely chopped

250 g (9 oz) flat mushrooms, sliced

200 g (7 oz) tin chopped tomatoes

¼ teaspoon sugar

20 g (¾ oz) butter, extra

20 g (¾ oz) plain (all purpose) flour

250 ml (9 fl oz/1 cup) milk

½ egg, lightly beaten

20 g (¾ oz) grated parmesan cheese

Preheat the oven to 220°C (425°F/Gas 7). Line a large baking tray with foil and brush with oil. Put the aubergine and potato in a single layer on the tray and sprinkle with salt and pepper. Bake for 20 minutes.

Melt the butter in a large frying pan over medium heat. Add the onion and cook, stirring, for 3–4 minutes, or until soft. Add the garlic and cook for 1 minute, or until fragrant. Increase the heat to high, add the mushrooms and stir continuously for 2–3 minutes, or until soft. Add the tomato, reduce the heat and simmer rapidly for 8 minutes, or until reduced. Stir in the sugar.

Melt the extra butter in a large saucepan over low heat. Add the flour and cook for 1 minute, or until pale and foaming. Remove from the heat and gradually stir in the milk. Return to the heat and stir constantly until it boils and thickens. Reduce the heat and simmer for 2 minutes. Remove from the heat and, when the bubbles subside, stir in the egg and parmesan.

Reduce the oven to 180°C (350°F/Gas 4). Grease a shallow 1.5 litre (48 fl oz) ovenproof dish. Spoon one-third of the mushroom mixture into the dish. Cover with potato and top with half the remaining mushrooms, then the aubergine. Finish with the remaining mushrooms, pour on the sauce and smooth the top. Bake for 30–35 minutes, or until the edges bubble. Leave for 10 minutes before serving.

EASY! · 80 MINUTES · SERVES 4

VEGETABLE CASSEROLE
WITH HERB DUMPLINGS

Heat the oil in a large saucepan and add the onion. Cook over low heat, stirring occasionally, for 5 minutes, or until soft. Add the garlic and paprika and cook, stirring, for 1 minute.

Add the potato, carrot, tomato and stock to the pan. Bring to the boil, then reduce the heat and simmer, covered, for 10 minutes. Add the sweet potato, broccoli and courgette and simmer for 10 minutes, or until tender. Preheat the oven to 200°C (400°F/Gas 6).

To **make** the dumplings, sift the flour and a pinch of salt into a bowl and add the butter. Rub the butter into the flour with your fingertips until it resembles fine breadcrumbs. Stir in the herbs and make a well in the centre. Add the milk, and mix with a flat-bladed knife, using a cutting action, until the mixture comes together in beads. Gather up the dough and lift onto a lightly floured surface, then divide into eight portions. Shape each portion into a ball.

Add the sour cream to the casserole. Pour into a 1 litre (35 fl oz/4 cups) ovenproof dish and top with the dumplings. Bake for 20 minutes, or until the dumplings are golden and a skewer comes out clean when inserted in the centre.

$1/2$ tablespoon olive oil

1 small onion, chopped

1 garlic clove , crushed

1 teaspoon sweet paprika

1 small potato, chopped

1 small carrot, sliced

200 g (7 oz) tin chopped tomatoes

(180 ml (6 fl oz/$3/4$ cup) vegetable stock

200 g ($6^1/2$ oz) orange sweet potato, cubed

75 g ($2^1/2$ oz) broccoli, cut into florets

1 courgette, thickly sliced

60 g (2 oz) self-raising flour

10 g ($1/4$ oz) cold butter, cut into small cubes

1 teaspoon chopped fresh flat-leaf parsley

$1/2$ teaspoon fresh thyme

$1/2$ teaspoon chopped fresh rosemary

80 ml ($2^1/2$ fl oz/$1/2$ cup) milk

1 tablespoon sour cream

REALLY EASY!   80 MINUTES   SERVES 2

MEDITERRANEAN VEGETABLE HOTPOT

1¹/2 tablespoons olive oil

1 small onion, chopped

1 garlic clove, crushed

¹/2 green pepper (capsicum), chopped

¹/2 red pepper (capsicum), chopped

1 large courgette (zucchini), sliced

1¹/2 slender aubergine (eggplant), sliced

1 cup (220 g/7³/4 oz) long-grain rice

125 ml (4 fl oz/¹/2 cup) white wine

50 g (1³/4 oz) button mushrooms, sliced

375 ml (6 fl oz/1¹/2 cups) vegetable stock

200 g (7 oz) tin chopped tomatoes

1 tablespoon tomato paste

75 g (2¹/2 oz) feta cheese

Like most hotpots and casseroles, this is best made a day in advance to let the flavours develop.

Heat the oil in a large heavy-based pan and cook the onion over medium heat for about 10 minutes, or until very soft but not browned. Add the garlic and cook for a further minute.

Add the green and red peppers and cook, stirring, for 3 minutes, Add the courgette and courgette and stir-fry for a further 5 minutes. Add the rice and stir-fry for 2 minutes.

Add the wine, mushrooms, stock, chopped tomatoes and tomato paste. Stir to combine. Bring to the boil, reduce the heat, cover and simmer for 20 minutes. The rice should be tender. Serve immediately, topped with the crumbled feta cheese.

REALLY EASY!   1 HOUR   SERVES 2

POTATO GRATIN

For something different, try combining potato and orange sweet potato, layering alternately. For extra flavour, add chopped fresh herbs to the cream and milk mixture.

Heat the butter in a frying pan and cook the onion over low heat for 5 minutes, or until it is soft and translucent.

Preheat the oven to 160°C (315°F/Gas 3). Grease the base and sides of a deep 1 litre (35 fl oz) ovenproof dish. Layer the potato slices with the onion and cheese (reserving 2 tablespoons of cheese for the top). Whisk together the cream and milk, and season with salt and cracked black pepper. Slowly pour over the potato, then sprinkle with the remaining cheese.

Bake for 50–60 minutes, or until golden brown and the potato is very soft. Leave to rest for 10 minutes before serving.

15 g ($^1/_2$ oz) butter

1 small onion, halved and thinly sliced

325 g (11 oz) floury potatoes, thinly sliced

45 g (1$^1/_2$ oz/$^1/_3$ cup) grated cheddar cheese

150 ml (5 fl oz) cream

50 ml (1$^1/_2$ fl oz) milk

REALLY EASY!

1$^1/_2$ HOURS

SERVES 2

PEANUT AND POTATO CURRY

1¹/₂ tablespoons oil

1¹/₂ garlic cloves, finely chopped

1 red chilli, finely chopped

1 teaspoon ground coriander

1 teaspoon ground cumin

pinch each of ground cinnamon and nutmeg

1 onion, chopped

750 g (1 lb 10 oz) potatoes, cubed

60 g (2¹/₄ oz) dry roasted peanuts, chopped

250 g (9 oz) ripe tomatoes, chopped

¹/₂ teaspoon soft brown sugar

1 teaspoon finely grated lime zest

1 tablespoon lime juice

coriander (cilantro) leaves and roughly chopped peanuts, to garnish

Add a ¹/₄ teaspoon of ground fenugreek seed to the spice mix for an outstandingly different flavour.

Heat the oil in a large, deep pan or wok and stir-fry the garlic, chilli and spices over low heat for 3 minutes, or until very fragrant. Add the onion and cook for another 3 minutes.

Add the potato to the pan, tossing to coat with the spice mixture. Add 125 ml (4 fl oz/¹/₂ cup) water, cover and cook over low heat for 10 minutes, stirring regularly.

Add the peanuts and tomato, uncover and simmer for 1 hour 10 minutes, stirring occasionally. Season with the sugar, zest, juice and salt and pepper. Garnish with coriander and peanuts. Serve with rice.

EASY! | 2 HOURS | SERVES 2 | VEGAN

SPICY BEANS ON BAKED SWEET POTATO

Preheat the oven to 210°C (415°F/Gas 6–7). Rinse the sweet potatoes, then pierce with a small sharp knife. Place it on a baking tray and bake for 1–1½ hours, or until soft when tested with a skewer or sharp knife.

Meanwhile, **heat** the oil in a large saucepan and cook the onion over medium heat for about 5 minutes, stirring occasionally, until very soft and golden. Add the garlic and spices, and cook, stirring, for 1 minute.

Add the tomato and stock, stir well, then add the vegetables and beans. Bring to the boil, then reduce the heat and simmer, partially covered, for 20 minutes. Uncover, increase the heat slightly, and cook for a further 10–15 minutes, or until the liquid has reduced and thickened. Stir in the coriander leaves just before serving.

To serve, **cut** the sweet potato in half lengthways. Spoon the vegetable mixture over the top. Add a dollop of sour cream and sprinkle with grated cheddar cheese.

REALLY EASY! · 1¾ HOURS · SERVES 2 · VEGAN

1 orange sweet potato

2 teaspoons olive oil

½ onion

1 garlic clove

1 teaspoon ground cumin

½ teaspoon ground coriander

¼ teaspoon chilli powder

135 (4¾ oz) tinned chopped tomatoes

80ml (⅓ cup) vegetable stock

1 small courgette (zucchini)

½ green pepper (capsicum)

100 g (3½ oz) tinned corn kernels

270 g (9½ oz) tinned red kidney beans

1 tablespoon chopped fresh coriander (cilantro) leaves

sour cream and grated cheddar cheese, to serve

DRY POTATO AND PEA CURRY

1 teaspoon brown
mustard seeds

1 tablespoon oil

1 onion, sliced

1 garlic clove, crushed

1 teaspoon grated
fresh ginger

$1/2$ teaspoon
ground turmeric

$1/4$ teaspoon chilli powder

$1/2$ teaspoon
ground cumin

$1/2$ teaspoon
garam masala

375 g (13 oz)
potatoes, cubed

50 g ($1^3/4$ oz) peas

1 tablespoon
chopped mint

It doesn't sound very appetising but you will love this one.

Heat the mustard seeds in a dry pan until they start to pop. Add the oil, onion, garlic and ginger and cook, stirring, until the onion is soft.

Add the turmeric, chilli powder, cumin, garam masala and potato, and season with salt and pepper. Stir until the potato is coated with the spice mixture. Add 60 ml (2 fl oz/$1/4$ cup) water and simmer, covered, for about 15–20 minutes, or until the potato is just tender. Stir occasionally to stop the curry sticking to the bottom of the pan.

Add the peas and stir until well combined. Simmer, covered, for 3–5 minutes, or until the potato is cooked and all the liquid is absorbed. Stir in the mint and season well.

REALLY EASY!

40 MINUTES

SERVES 2

VEGAN

SPICY VEGETABLE STEW WITH DHAL

To make the dhal, **put** the split peas in a bowl, cover with water and soak for 2 hours. Drain. Place in a large saucepan with the ginger, garlic, chilli and 375 ml (13 fl oz/1½ cups) water. Bring to the boil, reduce the heat and simmer for 45 minutes, or until soft.

Score a cross in the base of the tomato, soak in boiling water for 30 seconds, then plunge into cold water and peel the skin away from the cross. Deseed and roughly chop.

Heat the oil in a large saucepan. Cook the spices over medium heat for 30 seconds, or until fragrant. Add the onion and cook for 2 minutes, or until the onion is soft. Stir in the tomato, aubergine, carrot and cauliflower.

Add the dhal and stock, mix together well and simmer, covered, for 45 minutes, or until the vegetables are tender. Stir occasionally. Add the aubergine and peas during the last 10 minutes of cooking. Stir in the coriander leaves and serve hot.

REALLY EASY! | 2 HOURS + SOAKING TIME | SERVES 2 | VEGAN

Dhal

80 g (2¾ oz) yellow split peas

2.5 cm (1 inch) piece of ginger, grated

1 garlic clove, crushed

½ red chilli, seeded and chopped

1 large tomato

1 tablespoon oil

½ teaspoon yellow mustard seeds

½ teaspoon cumin seeds

½ teaspoon ground cumin

¼ teaspoon garam masala

1 small red onion, cut into thin wedges

1 large aubergine (eggplant), thickly sliced

1 carrot, thickly sliced

¼ small cauliflower, cut into florets

180 ml (6 fl oz) vegetable stock

1 small courgette (zucchini), thickly sliced

45 g /1½ oz/¼ cup) frozen peas

2 tablespoons fresh coriander (cilantro) leaves

MEXICAN TOMATO BAKE

3 ripe tomatoes

1 red onion

1/2 green pepper
(capsicum)

1 tablespoon oil

1 garlic clove, crushed

1/2 tablespoon
red wine vinegar

1/2 teaspoon sugar

1/4 teaspoon chilli powder

180 g (6 1/2 oz) tinned corn
kernels, drained

60 g (2 1/4 oz) plain
corn chips

75 g (2 3/4 oz/3/4 cups)
grated cheddar cheese

125 g (4 1/2 oz/1/2 cup)
sour cream

snipped chives, to garnish

Score a cross in the base of each tomato. Put in a heatproof bowl and cover with boiling water. Leave for 30 seconds, then transfer to cold water, drain and peel away the skin from the cross. Cut the tomatoes in half, scoop out the seeds and chop the flesh. Chop the onion. Cut the pepper in half, remove the seeds and membrane and chop. Preheat the oven to 160°C (315°F/Gas 2–3).

To **make** the sauce, heat the oil in a saucepan. Add the onions and garlic and cook over medium heat for 3 minutes. Add the tomato, pepper, vinegar, sugar and chilli. Cook, uncovered, for 6–7 minutes, or until the tomato is soft and the liquid has evaporated. Stir in the corn kernels over heat for 3 minutes.

Arrange layers of corn chips, sauce and cheese in an ovenproof dish, finishing with a cheese layer.

Spread with the sour cream. Bake, uncovered, for 15 minutes. Sprinkle with chives before serving.

REALLY EASY! · 55 MINUTES · SERVES 2

CURRIED LENTILS

Rinse the lentils and drain well. Place the lentils, stock and turmeric in a large heavy-based pan. Bring to the boil, reduce the heat and simmer, covered, for 10 minutes, or until just tender. Stir occasionally and check the mixture is not catching on the bottom of the pan.

Meanwhile, **heat** the ghee in a small frying pan and add the onion. Cook until soft and golden and add the garlic, chilli, cumin and coriander. Cook, stirring, for 2–3 minutes until fragrant. Stir the onions and spices into the lentil mixture and then add the tomato. Simmer over very low heat for 5 minutes, stirring frequently.

Season to taste and add the coconut milk. Stir until heated through. Serve with naan bread or rice.

REALLY EASY!

45 MINUTES

SERVES 2

---

125 g (4 oz/$^1/_2$ cup) red lentils

250 ml (8 fl oz/1 cup) vegetable stock

$^1/_4$ teaspoon ground turmeric

25 g ($^3/_4$ oz) ghee

1 small onion, chopped

1 garlic clove , finely chopped

1 small green chilli, seeded and finely chopped

1 teaspoon ground cumin

1 teaspoon ground coriander

1 tomato, chopped

60 ml (2 fl oz/$^1/_4$ cup) coconut milk

STIR-FRIES,
SALADS AND
VEGETABLES

INTRODUCTION

Fresh vegetables will make a difference to any dish so always shop little and often if you can. Always buy vegetables that look fresh and crisp and have a bright natural colour.

If you can't find fresh ingredients don't be tempted to buy that sad-looking specimen — wait until it is back in season and choose another recipe.

Freshness is important, especially in green leafy vegetables with a high water content, such as lettuces and spinach, because vitamin losses begin soon after picking.

Once back at college you need to store your vegetables correctly. Most vegetables benefit from being stored in a cool, dark place. Generally vegetables keep best when stored in the crisper section of the fridge. Store them unwashed and loosely packed in plastic bags. Squeeze the air out of the bags before storing.

Potatoes should not be placed in the fridge as they can develop a sweetish taste. Place in a paper bag and keep in a cool, dark, dry place with good ventilation. Properly stored they should remain in good condition for two months or more.

STIR-FRIED SPINACH
WITH TOFU AND ASIAN GREENS

1 tablespoon lime juice

1¹/₂ tablespoon vegetable oil

³/₄ tablespoon vegetarian fish sauce

¹/₂ teaspoon sambal oelek

¹/₂ teaspoon light brown sugar

100 g (3¹/₂ oz) smoked tofu

200 g (7 oz/¹/₂ bunch) choy sum (Chinese flowering cabbage)

75 g (2³/₄ oz) torn English spinach

1 teaspoon toasted sesame seeds

1 tablespoon coriander (cilantro) leaves

Tofu is also known as bean curd and is made from yellow soy beans which are soaked, ground and mixed with water then briefly cooked before being solidified. It is rich in protein yet low in fat and cholesterol.

To **make** the dressing, put lime juice, 1 tablespoon of the oil, fish sauce, sambal oelek and light brown sugar in a bowl and whisk well.

Cut the smoked tofu into 1.5–2 cm (⁵/₈–³/₄ inch) cubes. Trim the choy sum and cut it into 7–8 cm (2³/₄–3¹/₄ inch) lengths. Heat the remaining oil in a large wok over medium heat and gently stir-fry the tofu for 2–3 minutes, or until golden brown. Add half the dressing and toss to coat. Remove from the wok and set aside.

Add the choy sum to the wok and stir-fry for 1 minute. Addthe spinach and stir-fry for 1 minute. Return the tofu to the wok, add the sesame seeds and the remaining dressing and toss lightly.

Serve with coriander leaves piled on top.

REALLY EASY!

20 MINUTES

SERVES 2

ORANGE SWEET POTATO, SPINACH AND WATER CHESTNUT STIR-FRY

The strange-sounding sambal oelek is made from mashed fresh red chillies mixed with salt and vinegar or tamarind. Palm sugar is available from most large supermarkets in jars or wrapped in paper. But if you can't find any you can use demerara or soft brown sugar instead.

Bring a large saucepan of water to the boil. Add the rice and cook for 12 minutes, stirring occasionally. Drain well.

Meanwhile, **cut** the sweet potato into 1.5 cm x 1.5 cm (5/8 inch x 5/8 inch) cubes and cook in a large saucepan of boiling water for 15 minutes, or until tender. Drain well.

Heat a wok until very hot, add the oil and swirl to coat. Stir-fry the garlic and sambal oelek for 1 minute, or until fragrant. Add the sweet potato and water chestnuts and stir-fry over medium–high heat for 2 minutes. Reduce the heat to medium, add the palm sugar and cook for a further 2 minutes, or until the sugar has melted. Add the spinach, soy sauce and stock and toss until the spinach has just wilted. Serve on a bed of steamed rice.

150 g (5½ oz/¾ cup) long-grain rice

250 g (9 oz) orange sweet potato

½ tablespoon oil

1 garlic clove, crushed

1 teaspoon sambal oelek

110 g (3¾ oz) tin water chestnuts, sliced

1 teaspoon grated palm sugar (jaggery)

200 g (7 oz) English spinach, stems removed

1 tablespoon soy sauce

1 tablespoon vegetable stock

REALLY EASY! · 22 MINUTES · SERVES 2 · VEGAN

SNAKE BEANS STIR-FRIED
WITH THAI BASIL, GARLIC AND CHILLI

1^1/$_2$ tablespoons
soy sauce

30 ml (1 fl oz)
vegetable stock

1 tablespoon vegetable oil

^{1}/$_2$ teaspoon vegetarian
red curry paste

^{1}/$_2$ red Asian shallot,
finely chopped

1 garlic clove, finely sliced

^{1}/$_2$ small red chilli, seeds
removed and sliced

250 g (9 oz) snake beans,
cut into 8 cm (3 inch)
lengths on the diagonal

2 tablespoons Thai
basil leaves

Combine the soy sauce, stock and 1^1/$_2$ tablespoons (^{3}/$_4$ fl oz) water and set aside.

Heat a wok over high heat, add the vegetable oil, red curry paste, shallot, garlic and chilli and stir-fry until fragrant. Add the snake beans and cook for 5 minutes. Stir in the sauce and cook, tossing gently, until the beans are tender. Remove from the heat and season well. Stir in half the basil and scatter the rest on top as a garnish. Serve immediately.

REALLY EASY! | 25 MINUTES | SERVES 2 | VEGAN

CHILLI NOODLE AND NUT STIR-FRY

Chilli sauce is a bright-red hot sauce made from chillies, vinegar, sugar and salt. It can be used as a dipping sauce for foods that have been deep-fried but is sometimes used as an ingredient as in this recipe. If the sauce you have tastes too strong try diluting it with a little hot water.

Heat the wok over low heat, add the oils and swirl them to coat the side. When the oil is warm, add the chilli and heat until the oil is very hot.

Add the onion and garlic, and stir-fry for 1 minute, or until the onion just softens. Add the pepper, carrot and beans, and stir-fry for 1 minute. Add the celery, honey and 1 tablespoon water, and season with salt and pepper. Toss well, then cover and cook for 1–2 minutes, or until the vegetables are just tender.

Add the noodles and nuts and toss well. Cook, covered, for 1–2 minutes, or until the noodles are heated through. Stir in the garlic chives and serve, drizzled with the sweet chilli sauce and sesame oil.

REALLY EASY!

35 MINUTES

SERVES **2**

$^3/_4$ tablespoon oil

$^1/_2$ tablespoon sesame oil

2 small red chillies, finely chopped

1 small onion, cut into thin wedges

2 garlic cloves, very thinly sliced

$^1/_2$ red pepper (capsicum), cut into strips

$^1/_2$ green pepper (capsicum), cut into strips

1 large carrot, cut into batons

50 g ($1^3/_4$ oz) green beans

1 celery stalk, cut into batons

1 teaspoon honey

250 g (9 oz) Hokkien noodles, gently separated

50 g ($1^3/_4$ oz) dry-roasted peanuts

50 g ($1^3/_4$ oz) honey-roast cashews

15 g ($^1/_2$ oz) chopped fresh garlic chives, or 2 spring onions (scallions), chopped

sweet chilli sauce and sesame oil, to serve

PUMPKIN AND CASHEW STIR-FRY

oil, for cooking

75 g (2 1/2 oz) raw cashews

1/2 leek, white part only, sliced

1 teaspoon ground coriander

1 teaspoon ground cumin

1 teaspoon brown mustard seeds

1 garlic clove, crushed

500g (1 lb) butternut pumpkin, cubed

90 ml (3 fl oz) orange juice

1/2 teaspoon soft brown sugar

Heat the wok until very hot, add 1 tablespoon of the oil and swirl to coat. Stir-fry the cashews until golden, then drain on paper towels. Stir-fry the leek for 2–3 minutes, or until softened. Remove from the wok.

Reheat the wok, add 1 tablespoon of the oil and stir-fry the coriander, cumin, mustard seeds and garlic for 2 minutes, or until the spices are fragrant and the mustard seeds begin to pop. Add the pumpkin and stir to coat well. Stir-fry for 5 minutes, or until the pumpkin is brown and tender.

Add the orange juice and sugar. Bring to the boil and cook for 5 minutes. Add the leek and three-quarters of the cashews and toss well. Top with the remaining cashews.

REALLY EASY! · 35 MINUTES · SERVES 2 · VEGAN

ALMOND AND BROCCOLI STIR-FRY

This is one of those wonderful dishes that can be prepared two hours in advance of cooking. That means more time with your friends and guests; or soaking time in the bath!

Lightly **crush** the coriander seeds with a mortar and pestle or with a rolling pin. Cut the broccoli into small florets.

Heat the oil in a wok or a large heavy-based frying pan. Add the coriander seeds and almonds. Stir quickly over medium heat for 1 minute or until the almonds are golden.

Add the garlic, ginger and broccoli to the pan. Stir-fry over high heat for 2 minutes. Remove the pan from the heat. Pour the combined vinegar, sauce and oil into the pan. Toss until the broccoli is well coated. Serve immediately, sprinkled with toasted sesame seeds.

$1/2$ teaspoon coriander seeds

250 g (9 oz) broccoli

$1^1/2$ tablespoons olive oil

1 tablespoon slivered almonds

1 garlic clove, crushed

$1/2$ teaspoon finely shredded fresh ginger

1 tablespoon red wine vinegar

$1/2$ tablespoon soy sauce

1 teaspoon sesame oil

$1/2$ teaspoon toasted sesame seeds

REALLY EASY! — 15 MINUTES — SERVES 2 — VEGAN

BALTI AUBERGINE AND TOFU STIR-FRY

1 tablespoon oil

1 small onion,
finely chopped

35 g (1¼ oz) balti
curry paste

150 g (5½ oz) slender
aubergine (eggplant),
cut diagonally into
1 cm (½ inch) slices

150 g (5½ oz) firm
tofu, cut into 1.5 cm
(⅝ inch) cubes

2 small ripe tomatoes,
cut into wedges

30 ml (1 fl oz)
vegetable stock

35 g (1¼ oz) baby
English spinach leaves

25 g (1 oz) toasted
cashews

saffron rice, to serve

Remember that for a successful stir-fry you must heat the oil until it is very hot. Add the ingredients, and using a large, long-handled wooden spoon, continually toss and stir the food in the hot pan. The heat is greatest at the base of the pan and so by tossing and stirring the food, all sides of the wok are quickly sealed and all the juices and flavours are kept in.

Heat a wok or deep frying pan until very hot. Add the oil and swirl to coat. Add the onion and stir-fry over high heat for 3–4 minutes, or until softened and golden.

Stir in the balti curry paste and cook for 1 minute. Add the aubergine and cook for 5 minutes. Stir in the tofu, gently tossing for 3–4 minutes, or until golden.

Add the tomato and stock and cook for 3 minutes, or until the tomato is soft. Stir in the spinach and cook for 1–2 minutes, or until wilted. Season. Sprinkle the cashews over the top and serve with saffron rice.

REALLY EASY!   **35** MINUTES   SERVES **2**   VEGAN

TOFU AND SNOW PEA STIR-FRY

Kecap manis is an Indonesian sweet soy sauce. If you are unable to find it, use soy sauce sweetened with a little soft brown sugar. Sambal oelek is a Southeast Asian chilli paste.

Cut the tofu into 2 cm (³/₄ inch) cubes. Slice the mushrooms. Heat a wok over high heat, add 2 tablespoons of the peanut oil and swirl to coat the base and side of the wok. Add the tofu in two batches and stir-fry each batch for 2–3 minutes, or until lightly browned on all sides, then transfer to a plate.

Heat the remaining oil in the wok, add the sambal oelek, garlic, snow peas, mushrooms and 1 tablespoon water and stir-fry for 1–2 minutes, or until the vegetables are almost cooked but still crunchy. Return the tofu to the wok, add the kecap manis and stir-fry for 1 minute, or until heated through. Serve immediately with steamed rice.

REALLY EASY!

25 MINUTES

SERVES 2

VEGAN

300 g (10¹/₂ oz) firm tofu, drained

200 g (7 oz) fresh Asian mushrooms (such as shiitake or oyster)

30 ml (1 fl oz) peanut oil

1 teaspoon sambal oelek or chilli paste

1 garlic clove, finely chopped

150 g (5¹/₂ oz) snow peas (mangetout), trimmed

30 ml (1 fl oz) kecap manis

GREEN STIR-FRY WITH SESAME AND SOY

1 tablespoon light soy sauce

$^1/_2$ tablespoon hoisin sauce

$^1/_2$ tablespoon vegetable stock

1 tablespoon vegetable oil

$^1/_2$ teaspoon sesame oil

2 garlic cloves, finely sliced

1 teaspoon julienned ginger

1 kg (2 bunches) baby bok choy (pak choy), cut into quarters, well washed and drained

100 g (3$^1/_2$ oz) snowpeas (mangetout), trimmed

100 g (3$^1/_2$ oz) sugar snap peas, trimmed

1 tablespoon bamboo shoots, julienned

jasmine rice, to serve

In a small jug **mix** together the light soy sauce, hoisin sauce and stock.

Heat a wok over high heat and add the vegetable and sesame oils.

Stir-fry the garlic, ginger and bok choy for 3 minutes. Add the snowpeas, sugar snap peas and bamboo shoots and stir-fry for a further 5 minutes. Pour in the sauce, and gently toss until the sauce has reduced slightly to coat the just tender vegetables. Serve immediately with jasmine rice.

REALLY EASY! · 15 MINUTES · SERVES 2 · VEGAN

SESAME TOFU STIR-FRY

Soy sauce is made by fermenting soy beans with flour and water. It is then aged and distilled to make the resulting sauce. There are two types of soy sauce — light and dark. Generally the light sauce is used for cooking and the dark one for dipping.

Drain the tofu and pat dry with paper towels. Cut into cubes, place in a glass or ceramic bowl and add the sesame oil and soy sauce. Stir well and leave in the fridge to marinate for 30 minutes, stirring occasionally.

Heat the wok until very hot, add the sesame seeds and dry-fry until lightly golden. Tip onto a plate to cool.

Reheat the wok, add the oil and swirl it around to coat the side. Remove the tofu from the dish with a slotted spoon and reserve the marinade. Stir-fry the tofu over high heat, turning occasionally, for about 3 minutes, or until browned. Remove from the wok and set aside.

Add the vegetables and garlic, and cook, stirring often, until they are just tender. Add the rice and tofu, and stir-fry until heated through.

Add the toasted sesame seeds, the reserved marinade and extra soy sauce to taste. Toss to coat the tofu and vegetables, then serve immediately.

150 g (5$^{1}/_{2}$ oz) firm tofu

1 teaspoon sesame oil

1 tablespoon soy sauce

$^{1}/_{2}$ tablespoon sesame seeds

1 tablespoon oil

1$^{1}/_{2}$ courgette (zucchini), sliced

75 g (2$^{1}/_{2}$ oz) button mushrooms, halved or quartered

1 small red pepper (capsicum), cut into squares

1 garlic clove, crushed

225 g (8 oz) cold, cooked brown rice

1 tablespoon soy sauce, extra

REALLY EASY!

30 MINUTES + MARINATING TIME

SERVES 2

VEGAN

TEMPEH STIR-FRY

Coriander is sometimes called Chinese Parsley or Cilantro. There is really no substitute for it in recipes such as this one. Remember that you can use all of the coriander plant — leaves, stem, roots and seeds. The thick brown oyster sauce adds a delicious salty flavour to this stir-fry.

Heat the oils in a wok over high heat, add the garlic, ginger, chilli and spring onion and cook for 1–2 minutes, or until the onion is soft. Add the tempeh and cook for 5 minutes, or until golden. Remove and keep warm.

Add half the greens and 1 tablespoon water to the wok and cook, covered, for 3–4 minutes, or until wilted. Remove and repeat with the remaining greens and more water.

Return the greens and tempeh to the wok, add the sauce and vinegar and warm through. Top with the coriander and nuts. Serve with rice.

REALLY EASY!

15 MINUTES

SERVES 2

VEGAN

$^1/_2$ teaspoon sesame oil

$^1/_2$ tablespoon peanut oil

1 garlic clove, crushed

$^1/_2$ tablespoon grated fresh ginger

1 small red chilli, finely sliced

2 spring onions (scallions), sliced on the diagonal

150 g (5$^1/_2$ oz) tempeh, diced

250 g (9 oz) baby bok choy (pak choy) leaves

400 g (14 oz) Chinese broccoli, chopped

60 ml (2 fl oz) mushroom oyster sauce

1 tablespoon rice vinegar

1 tablespoon fresh coriander (cilantro) leaves

1$^1/_2$ tablespoons toasted cashew nuts

SPICY BROCCOLI AND CAULIFLOWER STIR-FRY

1/2 teaspoon ground cumin

1/2 teaspoon ground coriander

1 tablespoon oil

1 garlic clove, crushed

1/2 teaspoon grated fresh ginger

1/4 teaspoon chilli powder

1 small onion, cut into wedges

100 g (3 1/2 oz) cauliflower, cut into bite-sized florets

100 g (3 1/2 oz) broccoli, cut into bite-sized florets

100 g (3 1/2 oz) haloumi cheese, diced

1/2 tablespoon lemon juice

Heat the wok until very hot, add the cumin and coriander, and dry-fry the spices for 1 minute. Add the oil with the garlic, ginger and chilli powder, and stir-fry briefly. Add the onion and cook for 2–3 minutes, being careful not to burn the spices.

Add the cauliflower and broccoli, and stir-fry until they are cooked through but still crisp. Add the haloumi and toss well until the haloumi is coated with the spices and is just beginning to melt. Season well and serve sprinkled with lemon juice.

REALLY EASY! · 25 MINUTES · SERVES 2

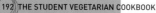

STIR-FRIED ASIAN GREENS AND MUSHROOMS

Remove any tough outer leaves from the Chinese broccoli and bok choy. Cut into 4 cm (1½ inch) pieces across the leaves, including the stems. Wash thoroughly, then drain and dry thoroughly. Wipe the mushrooms with a paper towel and trim the ends. Slice the shiitake mushrooms thickly.

Combine the soy sauce and palm sugar with 1½ tablespoons water. Set aside.

Heat the wok until very hot, add the oil and swirl it around to coat the sides. Stir-fry the spring onion, ginger, chilli and garlic over low heat for 30 seconds, without browning. Increase the heat to high and add the Chinese broccoli, bok choy and snow peas. Stir-fry for 1–2 minutes, or until the vegetables are wilted.

Add the prepared mushrooms and soy sauce mixture. Stir-fry over high heat for 1–2 minutes, or until the mushrooms and sauce are heated through. Serve immediately.

REALLY EASY!   25 MINUTES   SERVES 2   VEGAN

10 stems Chinese broccoli

2 baby bok choy (pak choy)

50 g (1¾ oz) shimeji or enoki mushrooms

50 g (1¾ oz) shiitake mushrooms

½ tablespoon soy sauce

1 teaspoon crushed palm sugar (jaggery)

½ tablespoon oil

2 spring onions, (scallions) cut into short pieces 5 cm (2 inch) fresh ginger, cut into thin strips

1 small red chilli, seeded and finely chopped

1 garlic clove, crushed

60 g (2 oz) snow peas, (mangetout) halved

SPINACH AND
SWEET POTATO SALAD
WITH ORANGE-SESAME DRESSING

1 small pitta bread

1 1/2 tablespoons olive oil

250 g (9 oz) orange sweet potato, unpeeled, cut into slices 1 cm (1/2 inch) thick

1 small orange

75 g (2 3/4 oz) baby English spinach

Dressing

1 1/2 tablespoons olive oil

1/2 teaspoon sesame oil

1 tablespoon orange juice

1/2 teaspoon lemon juice

1/2 teaspoon finely grated orange zest

1 garlic clove, crushed

1 teaspoon dijon mustard

Sweet potato and orange are one of those food combinations that are just meant to go together. Roasting or grilling sweet potato makes it tender and enhances its sweetness. This salad, with its contrast of sweet and tangy, soft and crisp, is easy but impressive.

Preheat a grill (broiler) to high. Cut off and discard the edge of the pitta bread, split the bread into 2 thin halves, and lightly brush all over with some of the oil. Place under the grill and toast until crisp and lightly browned. Reserve.

Toss the sweet potato in the remaining oil and grill until soft and golden on both sides, 8–10 minutes. Transfer to a salad bowl.

Peel the orange, removing all the pith. To fillet the segments, hold the orange over a bowl and use a sharp knife to cut down either side of the membranes. Put the segments in the bowl and add the spinach. Break up the pitta crisps into small shards and put into the bowl. Toss lightly.

To make the dressing, **put** all the ingredients in a small bowl and whisk to blend. Season with salt and freshly ground black pepper, to taste. Pour over the salad just before serving.

REALLY EASY!　35 MINUTES　SERVES 2　VEGAN

TUNISIAN AUBERGINE SALAD WITH PRESERVED LEMON

This salad is best made in advance and left for several hours for the flavours to merge.

Cut the aubergine into 2 cm ($^3/_4$ inch) cubes, put in a large colander and sprinkle with 1–2 teaspoons salt. Set aside to drain in the sink for 2–3 hours. Dry with paper towels.

Heat half the olive oil in a large flameproof casserole dish over medium–high heat. Fry the aubergine in batches for 5–6 minutes, or until golden, adding more oil as required. Drain on crumpled paper towels.

Reduce the heat and add any remaining oil to the casserole dish, along with the cumin, garlic, currants and almonds. Fry for 20–30 seconds, or until the garlic starts to colour. Add the tomato and oregano and cook for 1 minute. Remove from the heat.

Trim the zest from the piece of preserved lemon and cut the rind into thin strips. Discard the flesh.

Return the aubergine to the casserole and add the chilli, lemon juice, parsley and preserved lemon rind. Toss gently and season with freshly ground black pepper. Set aside at room temperature for at least 1 hour before serving. Check the seasoning, then drizzle with extra virgin olive oil.

1 large aubergine (eggplant)

60 ml (2 fl oz/$^1/_4$ cup) olive oil

$^1/_2$ teaspoon cumin seeds

1 garlic clove, very thinly sliced

$^1/_2$ tablespoon currants

$^1/_2$ tablespoon slivered almonds

3 small roma (plum) tomatoes, quartered lengthways

$^1/_2$ teaspoon dried oregano

2 red bird's eye chillies, halved lengthways and seeded

1 tablespoon lemon juice

2 tablespoons parsley, chopped

$^1/_4$ preserved or salted lemon

extra virgin olive oil, to serve

REALLY EASY!

40 MINUTES + STANDING TIME

SERVES 2

VEGAN

BABY BEETROOT
AND TATSOI SALAD WITH
HONEY MUSTARD DRESSING

800g (1 lb 12 oz/1 bunch) baby beetroot

large pinch of salt

125 g (4^1/$_2$ oz/^{3}/$_4$ cup) broad (fava) beans (from 125 g (9 oz/ 1^1/$_2$ cups) fresh broad beans in the pod)

small inner leaves of 100 g (3^1/$_2$ oz/^{1}/$_2$ bunch) tatsoi

40 ml (1^1/$_4$ fl oz) olive oil

^{1}/$_2$ tablespoon lemon juice

^{1}/$_2$ tablespoon wholegrain mustard

^{1}/$_2$ tablespoon honey

salt and freshly ground black pepper

I don't recommend the wearing of rubber gloves lightly but beetroot juice is one of the most difficult stains to remove, from your skin, from a work surface or, even worse, from your clothes. Treat it with great respect or see your rental deposit disappear in an instant!

Wearing rubber gloves, **trim** baby beetroot, discarding the stalks but reserving the unblemished leaves. Bring a medium saucepan of water to the boil. Add the beetroot and simmer, covered, for 8–10 minutes, or until tender, then drain.

Ease off the skins, pat dry with paper towels and rinse. Put the beetroot in a large shallow bowl. Bring a small saucepan of water to the boil. Add a large pinch of salt and the broad (fava) beans and simmer for 2–3 minutes, then drain. When cool enough to handle, slip the beans out of their skins and add to the beetroot. Add the reserved beetroot leaves and tatsoi.

To make the dressing, **put** the olive oil, lemon juice, wholegrain mustard and honey in a small bowl and whisk well to combine.

Season with salt and freshly ground black pepper, to taste. Pour over the beetroot mixture and toss gently. Serve warm or at room temperature.

REALLY EASY! 25 MINUTES SERVES 2 VEGAN

ASIAN-STYLE COLESLAW

Combine red cabbage and Chinese cabbage in a large bowl. Peel carrot and shave it with a vegetable peeler. Add the carrot, onion and chilli to the bowl, along with snow peas (mangetout), Thai (holy) basil and 1 tablespoon of the roasted peanuts and toss to combine.

To make the dressing, **put** all the dressing ingredients in a small bowl and whisk until combined. Pour over the cabbage mixture and toss well to coat.

Scatter remaining roasted peanuts on top. Serve at room temperature.

REALLY EASY! | **20** MINUTES | SERVES **2**

---

100 g (3$^{1}/_{2}$ oz) finely shredded red cabbage

85 g (3 oz/1 cup) Chinese cabbage, finely shredded

1 small carrot

$^{1}/_{2}$ red onion, thinly sliced

1 seeded small red chilli, cut lengthways

40 g (1$^{1}/_{2}$ oz/$^{1}/_{3}$ cup) snow peas (mangetout), thinly sliced

$^{1}/_{2}$ small handful Thai (holy) basil, torn

2 tablespoons coarsely chopped roasted peanuts

Dressing

1 tablespoon lime juice

$^{3}/_{4}$ teaspoon fresh ginger, finely grated

45 g (1$^{3}/_{4}$ oz) light sour cream

$^{1}/_{2}$ teaspoon vegetarian fish sauce

1 garlic clove, crushed

GADO GADO

1 small carrot, thinly sliced

50 g (1³/₄ oz) cauliflower, cut into small florets

30 g (1 oz) snowpeas (mangetout), trimmed

50 g (1³/₄ oz) bean sprouts

4 well-shaped iceberg lettuce leaves

2 small potatoes, cooked and cut into thin slices

¹/₂ Lebanese (short) cucumber, thinly sliced

1 hard-boiled egg, peeled and cut into quarters

1 ripe tomato, cut into wedges

Peanut sauce

¹/₂ tablespoon oil

¹/₂ small onion, finely chopped

60 g (2¹/₄ oz/¹/₄ cup) crunchy peanut butter

90 ml (3 fl oz/¹/₃ cup) coconut milk

¹/₂ teaspoon sambal oelek

¹/₂ tablespoon lemon juice

¹/₂ tablespoon kecap manis

This isn't one of my favourites, but then I'm not a great peanut lover! My college friends tell me it is divine and I am happy to take their word for it.

Steam the carrots and cauliflower in a saucepan for 5 minutes, or until nearly tender. Add the snowpeas and cook for 2 minutes. Add the bean sprouts and cook for a further 1 minute. Remove from the heat and cool.

To make the peanut sauce, **heat** the oil in a saucepan and cook the onion for 5 minutes over low heat, or until soft and lightly golden. Add the peanut butter, coconut milk, sambal oelek, lemon juice, kecap manis and 60 ml (2 fl oz/¹/₄ cup) water, and stir well. Bring to the boil, stirring constantly, then reduce the heat and simmer for 5 minutes, or until the sauce has reduced and thickened. Remove from the heat.

Place two lettuce leaves together (one inside the other) to make 4 lettuce cups. In each lettuce cup, arrange one quarter of the potato, carrot, cauliflower, snowpeas, bean sprouts and cucumber. Top with some of the peanut sauce, and garnish with the egg and tomato.

EASY! — 35 MINUTES — SERVES 2

WARM POTATO SALAD
WITH GREEN OLIVE DRESSING

Boil the potatoes for 15 minutes or until just tender (pierce with the tip of a sharp knife — if the potato comes away easily it is ready). Drain and cool slightly.

While the potatoes are cooking, **place** the olives and capers in a small bowl with the parsley, lemon juice, lemon zest, garlic and olive oil. Whisk with a fork to combine.

Cut the potatoes into halves and gently toss with the dressing while still warm. Taste before seasoning with fresh black pepper and a little salt, if required.

REALLY EASY! **30** MINUTES SERVES **2** VEGAN

500g (1 lb 2 oz) Nicola potatoes

30g (1 oz) green olives

1 teaspoon capers

1 small handful parsley

3 teaspoons lemon juice

$1/2$ teaspoon finely grated lemon zest

1 garlic clove

2 tablespoons olive oil

AUBERGINE AND LENTIL SALAD

30 ml (1 fl oz) olive oil

150 g (5¹/₄ oz) aubergine (eggplant), diced into 5 mm (¹/₄ inch) cubes

¹/₂ small red onion, finely diced

pinch ground cumin

1 garlic clove, chopped

100 g (3¹/₂ oz) puy lentils

180 ml (6 fl oz/³/₄ cup) vegetable stock

1 tablespoon chopped parsley

¹/₂ tablespoon red wine vinegar

¹/₂ tablespoon extra virgin olive oil

Puy lentils that are grown in the Le Puy region of France and are distinguished by their green and blue colour. I love their delicate peppery taste and, best of all, they retain their shape during cooking.

Heat 1 tablespoon of olive oil in a large frying pan over medium heat. Add the aubergine and cook, stirring constantly, for 5 minutes, or until soft. Add the onion and cumin and cook for another 2–3 minutes, or until the onion has softened. Place the mixture in a bowl and season well.

Heat the remaining olive oil in the frying pan over medium heat. Add the garlic and cook for 1 minute. Add the lentils and stock and cook, stirring regularly, over low heat for 40 minutes, or until the liquid has evaporated and the lentils are tender.

Add the lentils to the bowl with the aubergine and stir in the parsley and red wine vinegar. Season well with salt and black pepper, drizzle with the extra virgin olive oil and serve warm.

REALLY EASY! • 55 MINUTES • SERVES 2 • VEGAN

MOROCCAN **CARROT SALAD**
WITH GREEN OLIVES AND MINT

In a small frying pan, **dry-fry** the cumin and coriander seeds for 30 seconds or until fragrant. Cool and then grind in a mortar and pestle or spice grinder. Place into a large mixing bowl with the red wine vinegar, olive oil, garlic, harissa and orange flower water. Whisk to combine.

Blanch the carrots in boiling salted water for 5 minutes, until almost tender. Drain into a colander and allow to sit for a few minutes until they dry. While still hot, add to the red wine vinegar dressing, and toss gently to coat. Allow to cool to room temperature, for the dressing to infuse into the carrots. Add the green olives and mint. Season well and toss gently to combine.

Serve on the watercress leaves.

REALLY EASY! · 20 MINUTES · SERVES 2 · VEGAN

$3/4$ teaspoon cumin seeds

$1/4$ teaspoon coriander seeds

$1/2$ tablespoon red wine vinegar

1 tablespoon olive oil

1 garlic clove, crushed

1 teaspoon harissa

1 dash orange flower water

300 g (10$1/2$ oz) baby (dutch) carrots, tops trimmed, well scrubbed

20 g ($3/4$ oz) large green olives, pitted and finely sliced

1 tablespoon shredded mint

15 g ($1/2$ cup) picked watercress leaves

TOFU SALAD

1 teaspoon Thai
sweet chilli sauce

$1/4$ teaspoon grated
fresh ginger

1 garlic clove, crushed

1 teaspoon soy sauce

1 tablespoon oil

125 g ($4^1/2$ oz) firm tofu

50 g ($1^3/4$ oz) snow peas
(mange tout), cut into
3 cm ($1^1/4$ inch) lengths

1 small carrot,
cut into matchsticks

50 g ($1^3/4$ oz) red
cabbage, finely shredded

1 tablespoon
chopped peanuts

Place the chilli sauce, ginger, garlic, soy sauce and oil in a small screw-top jar and shake well. Cut the tofu into 2 cm ($3/4$ inch) cubes. Place the tofu in a medium non-metallic bowl, pour the marinade over and stir. Cover with plastic wrap and refrigerate for 1 hour.

Place the snow peas in a small pan, pour boiling water over and leave to stand for 1 minute, then drain and plunge into iced water. Drain well.

Add the snow peas, carrots and cabbage to tofu and toss lightly to combine. Transfer to a serving bowl or individual plates, sprinkle with peanuts and serve immediately.

REALLY EASY! · 20 MINUTES + MARINATING TIME · SERVES 2 · VEGAN

WARM CASARECCI AND SWEET POTATO SALAD

Cavatelli, farfalle, fusilli and gigli pasta may all be substituted for the casarecci pasta.

Preheat the oven to 200°C (400°F/Gas 6). Peel the sweet potato and cut into large pieces. Place in a baking dish, drizzle with the olive oil and season generously with salt and cracked black pepper. Bake for 20 minutes, or until the sweet potato is tender.

Meanwhile, **cook** the pasta in a large saucepan of rapidly boiling water until *al dente*. Drain well.

Drain the oil from the feta and whisk 3 tablespoons of the oil together with the balsamic vinegar to make a dressing.

Steam the asparagus until bright green and tender. Drain well.

Combine the pasta, sweet potato, asparagus, rocket, feta, chopped tomato and pine nuts in a bowl. Add the dressing and toss gently. Season with black pepper and serve immediately.

375 g (13 oz) orange sweet potato

1 tablespoon extra virgin olive oil

250 g (9 oz) casarecci pasta

160 g (5³/4 oz) marinated feta cheese in oil

1¹/2 tablespoons balsamic vinegar

75 g (¹/2 bunch) asparagus, cut into short lengths

50 g (1³/4 oz) baby rocket (arugula) or baby English spinach leaves

1 vine-ripened tomato, chopped

20 g (³/4 oz) pine nuts, toasted

REALLY EASY!

35 MINUTES

SERVES 2

CHERRY AND PEAR TOMATO SALAD
WITH WHITE BEANS

1 1/2 tablespoons olive oil

1 red Asian shallot,
finely diced

1/2 large garlic
clove, crushed

3/4 tablespoon
lemon juice

125 g (4 1/2 oz) red cherry
tomatoes, halved

125 g (4 1/2 oz) yellow
pear tomatoes, halved

200 g (7 oz) tin white
beans, drained and rinsed

2 tablespoons basil
leaves, torn

1 tablespoon
chopped parsley

Place the olive oil, diced shallots, crushed garlic and lemon juice into a small bowl and whisk to combine.

Place the halved cherry and pear tomatoes and the white beans in a serving bowl. Drizzle with the dressing and scatter the basil and parsley over the top. Toss gently to combine.

REALLY EASY!

15 MINUTES

SERVES 2

VEGAN

VIETNAMESE SALAD
WITH LEMONGRASS DRESSING

This may look a little daunting but it isn't! The kaffir lime leaves add a distinct flavour but if you can't find any at your local store use fresh young lime or lemon leaves. Make sure that you wash the lemongrass well before using. If you can't find lemon grass locally, substitute with the peel of half a lemon for one stalk of lemon grass.

Place the rice vermicelli in a bowl and cover with boiling water. Leave for 10 minutes, or until soft, then drain, rinse under cold water and cut into short lengths.

Place the vermicelli, mint, coriander, onion, mango, cucumber and three-quarters of the nuts in a large bowl and toss together.

To make the dressing, **place** all the ingredients in a jar with a lid and shake together.

Toss the dressing through the salad and refrigerate for 30 minutes. Sprinkle with the remaining nuts just before serving.

REALLY EASY! — 30 MINUTES + MARINATING TIME — SERVES 2 — VEGAN

100 g (3½ oz) dried rice vermicelli

2 tablespoons torn Vietnamese mint

3 tablespoons coriander (cilantro) leaves

¼ red onion, cut into thin wedges

½ green mango, cut into julienne strips

½ Lebanese (short) cucumber, halved lengthways and thinly sliced on the diagonal

70 g (½ cup) crushed peanuts

Lemongrass dressing

60 ml (¼ cup) lime juice

½ tablespoon shaved palm sugar

30 ml (1 oz) seasoned rice vinegar

1 stem lemongrass, finely chopped

1 small red chilli, seeded and finely chopped

2 makrut (kaffir) lime leaves, shredded

FATTOUSH SALAD

1/2 large pitta (Lebanese) bread, split

1 baby cos (romaine) lettuce, torn into bite-sized pieces

1 tomato, chopped

1 small Lebanese (short) cucumber, chopped

1/2 green pepper (capsicum), cut into large dice

2 spring onions (scallions), chopped

1 small handful mint, roughly chopped

1 small handful coriander (cilantro) leaves, roughly chopped

Dressing

1 1/2 tablespoon lemon juice

1 1/2 tablespoons olive oil

1/2 tablespoon sumac

Sumac is available in the spice section of many supermarkets and will add a tangy lemon flavour to this delicious salad

Preheat the oven to 180°C (350°F/Gas 4). Place the pitta bread on a baking tray and bake for 5 minutes, or until golden and crisp. Remove from the oven and cool. Break into 2 cm (3/4 inch) pieces.

To make the dressing, **mix** the lemon juice, oil and sumac together and season to taste.

In a serving bowl, **toss** the lettuce, tomatoes, cucumber, pepper, spring onions and herbs together. Crumble over the toasted pitta bread, drizzle with the dressing and serve immediately.

REALLY EASY! · **25** MINUTES · SERVES **2** · VEGAN

SWEETCORN
WITH LIME AND CHILLI BUTTER

I always offer plenty of paper towels with this dish, as the corn chunks are quite messy to eat.

Remove the skins and silky threads from the corn cobs. Wash well, then using a long sharp knife cut each cob into 2 cm (3/4 inch) chunks.

Heat the butter and oil in a large saucepan over low heat. Add the lemongrass and braise gently for 5 minutes, then remove from the pan. Add the chilli and cook for 2 minutes. Stir in the grated lime zest, lime juice, 1 1/2 tablespoons of water and the corn. Cover and cook, shaking the pan frequently, for 5–8 minutes, or until the corn is tender. Season well, then stir in the coriander and serve hot.

REALLY EASY! · 30 MINUTES · SERVES 2

2 corn cobs

25 g (3/4 oz) butter

1 tablespoon olive oil

1/2 stem lemongrass, bruised and cut in half

2 small bird's eye chillies, seeded and finely chopped

1 tablespoon lime zest, finely grated

1 tablespoon lime juice

1 tablespoon finely chopped coriander (cilantro) leaves

CAULIFLOWER CHEESE

250 g (9 oz) cauliflower, cut into pieces

15 g (¹/₂ oz) butter

15 g (¹/₂ oz) plain (all purpose) flour

155 ml (5 fl oz) warm milk

¹/₂ teaspoon dijon mustard

30 g (1 oz) grated cheddar cheese

30 g (1 oz) grated parmesan cheese

1 tablespoon fresh breadcrumbs

1¹/₂ tablespoon grated cheddar cheese, extra

Brush a 750ml (26 fl oz/3 cups) heatproof dish with melted butter or oil. Cook the cauliflower in lightly salted boiling water until just tender. Drain. Place in the dish and keep warm.

Melt the butter in a pan. Stir in the flour and cook for 1 minute, or until golden and bubbling. Remove from the heat and whisk in the milk and mustard. Return to the heat and bring to the boil, stirring constantly. Cook, stirring, over low heat for 2 minutes, then remove from the heat. Add the cheeses and stir until melted. Season with salt and white pepper and pour over the cauliflower.

Mix together the breadcrumbs and extra Cheddar cheese and sprinkle over the sauce. Grill until the top is browned and bubbling and then serve immediately.

REALLY EASY!   30 MINUTES   SERVES 2

ROSEMARY AND GARLIC
ROASTED POTATOES

Preheat the oven to 200°C (400°F/Gas 6). Cook the potatoes in a large saucepan of boiling salted water for 10 minutes, or until just tender. Drain in a colander, and sit for 5 minutes so they dry slightly.

Meanwhile, **pour** the olive oil into a large roasting tray, and heat in the oven for 5 minutes. Add the potatoes to the tray (they should sizzle in the hot oil), add the garlic and rosemary and season liberally with salt and pepper. Roast, stirring occasionally, so they cook evenly, for about 1 hour, or until golden and crisp.

Serve with the roasted garlic cloves popped from their skin and the rosemary leaves.

750 g (1lb 10 oz) potatoes, peeled and cut into large chunks

40 ml (1 1/4 oz) olive oil

6 garlic cloves in the skin, root end trimmed

1 tablespoon rosemary leaves

REALLY EASY!

80 MINUTES

SERVES **2**

VEGAN

MASHED CARROTS WITH CUMIN SEEDS

3 carrots

1/2 tablespoon olive oil

1 garlic clove,
finely chopped

1/2 teaspoon
ground turmeric

1 teaspoon finely grated
fresh ginger

30 g (1 oz) thick
Greek-style yoghurt

1 teaspoon prepared
harissa

1 tablespoon chopped
coriander (cilantro) leaves

1 teaspoon lime juice

1/2 teaspoon cumin seeds

Cumin is one of my favourite spices. It's unusual taste adds a wonderful flavour for which there is simply no substitute.

Peel the carrots and cut into 2.5 cm (1 inch) chunks. Place them in a large saucepan and cover with cold water. Bring to the boil, then reduce the heat and simmer for 3 minutes. Drain and allow to dry.

Heat the olive oil in a heavy-based, non-stick saucepan. Cook the garlic, ground turmeric and ginger over medium heat for 1 minute, or until fragrant. Add the carrots, and cook for 3 minutes. Stir in 1 tablespoon water and cook, covered, over low heat for 10–15 minutes, or until the carrots are soft. Transfer the mixture to a bowl and roughly mash.

Add the yoghurt, harissa, coriander and lime juice to the carrots and stir to combine. Season to taste with salt and freshly ground black pepper.

Heat a heavy-based frying pan, add the cumin seeds, and dry-fry for 1–2 minutes, or until fragrant. Scatter over the mashed carrots and serve.

REALLY EASY! · 40 MINUTES · SERVES 2

ROASTED RED ONION
AND ROMA TOMATOES WITH
BALSAMIC VINAIGRETTE

Try to pick roma tomatoes that are firm and smooth-skinned. Don't buy any tomato which has blotchy green or brown skin or any that feel soft, look wrinkled or that have broken skin.

Preheat the oven to 150°C (300°F/ Gas 2) and lightly brush a baking tray with oil.

Cut the tomatoes into quarters and arrange on the tray. Remove the tops of the onion and peel. Cut the onion into 8 wedges and place on the tray with the tomatoes. Place the garlic in the middle of the tray, spaced 5 cm (2 inches) apart and season all of the vegetables well. Roast for 1 hour.

Arrange the tomatoes and onion wedges on a serving plate. Peel the garlic and crush in a small bowl. Add the balsamic vinegar and mustard to the garlic and, using a small wire whisk, beat in the olive oil, adding it slowly in a thin stream. Season the dressing well and drizzle over the onions and tomatoes. Serve immediately.

oil, to brush

4 roma (plum) tomatoes

1 red onion

1 garlic clove

$3/4$ tablespoon balsamic vinegar

$1/2$ teaspoon French mustard

30 ml (1 oz) extra virgin olive oil

REALLY EASY! **70** MINUTES SERVES **2** VEGAN

GREEN BEANS WITH FETA AND TOMATOES

1/2 tablespoon olive oil

----

1 small onion, chopped

----

1 garlic clove, crushed

3/4 tablespoon chopped oregano

----

60 ml (2 fl oz/1/4 cup) white wine

----

210 g (71/2 oz) tin chopped tomatoes

----

125 g (41/2 oz) green beans, trimmed

1/2 tablespoon balsamic vinegar

----

100 g (31/2 oz) feta cheese, cut into 1.5 cm (5/8 inch) cubes

----

Heat the oil in a saucepan, add the onion and cook over medium heat for 3–5 minutes, or until soft. Add the garlic and half the oregano, and cook for another minute. Pour in the white wine and cook for 3 minutes, or until reduced by one-third.

Stir in the chopped tomato and cook, uncovered, for 10 minutes. Add the beans and cook, covered, for another 10 minutes.

Stir in the balsamic vinegar, feta and remaining oregano. Season with salt and pepper, and serve.

REALLY EASY! 45 MINUTES SERVES 2

CREAMED SPINACH

Remove the tough ends from the spinach stalks and wash the leaves well. Shake to remove any excess water from the leaves, but do not dry completely.

Melt the butter in a large frying pan. Add the crushed garlic and the spinach, season with nutmeg, salt and pepper, and cook over medium heat until the spinach is just wilted. Remove from the heat and place the spinach in a sieve. Press down well to squeeze out all of the excess moisture. Transfer to a chopping board and, using a mezzaluna or a sharp knife, chop the spinach finely.

Pour the cream into the frying pan and heat gently. Add the spinach to the pan and stir until warmed through. Arrange the spinach on a serving dish and sprinkle with the parmesan.

750 g (1 lb 10 oz) English spinach

1 teaspoon butter

1 garlic clove, crushed

pinch freshly grated nutmeg

40 ml (1 fl oz) thick (double/heavy) cream

$1/2$ tablespoon grated parmesan cheese

REALLY EASY!

15 MINUTES

SERVES **2**

BAKED FENNEL WITH A GRANA CRUST

2 bulbs fennel, trimmed

seasoned plain
(all-purpose) flour
for dusting

125 ml (4$^1/_2$ fl oz/
$^1/_2$ cup) milk

1 pinch ground nutmeg

40 g (1$^1/_2$ oz) butter

25 g (1 oz/$^1/_4$ cup)
Grana Padano cheese
finely grated

This is a wonderful way to prepare fennel. It is a simple variation on the traditional gratinée, still using cheese, milk and butter — all of which go so well with the aniseed taste of fennel — but in much smaller amounts.

Preheat the oven to 180°C (350°F/Gas 4). Grease a medium, shallow ovenproof dish. Bring a large saucepan of water to the boil and add 1 teaspoon salt and the whole fennel bulbs. Simmer for 12–15 minutes, or until just tender. Drain and cut each bulb length-ways into quarters, ensuring that each quarter is still attached at the stem.

Dust the fennel with the seasoned flour and lay them in a single layer in the prepared dish. Pour in the milk, sprinkle with nutmeg and dot the butter over the top. Sprinkle with the Grana Padano. Bake for 30 minutes, or until the cheese top is crusty, the fennel is fork tender and the milk forms a little sauce.

REALLY EASY! 55 MINUTES SERVES 2

PEPPERONATA

Slice the red and yellow peppers into 2 cm (^{3}/$_4$ inch) wide strips. Heat the oil in a large heavy-based frying pan and cook the onion over low heat for 5 minutes, or until softened. Add the pepper strips and cook for another 5 minutes. Add the tomatoes and cook, covered, over low–medium heat for 10 minutes, or until the vegetables are soft. Remove the lid and simmer for an extra 2 minutes.

Stir in the sugar and vinegar. Place in a serving bowl and scatter with the garlic and parsley. Season with salt and freshly ground black pepper.

REALLY EASY! · 35 MINUTES · SERVES 2 · VEGAN

2 small red peppers (capsicums)

2 small yellow peppers (capsicums)

1 tablespoon olive oil

1 small red onion, thinly sliced

2 small fresh tomatoes, finely chopped

^{1}/$_2$ tablespoon sugar

1 tablespoon balsamic vinegar

1 garlic clove, finely chopped

3 g (1 oz) flat-leaf (Italian) parsley, chopped

HONEY ROASTED ROOT VEGETABLES

30 g (1 oz) butter

1 tablespoon honey

2 thyme sprigs

2 small carrots, peeled and cut into chunks

1 parsnip, peeled and cut into chunks

1 small orange sweet potato, peeled and cut into chunks

1 small white sweet potato, peeled and cut into chunks

4 small pickling onions, peeled

4 Jerusalem artichokes, peeled

1/2 garlic head

The joy of this recipe is that it is so easy to prepare. Once made you pop it in the oven and forget about it. An hour later you have a hot, filling dish to warm every extremity.

Preheat the oven to 200°C (400°F/ Gas 6). Melt the butter in a medium ovenproof baking dish over medium heat. Add the honey and thyme and stir. Remove from the heat and add the carrot, parsnip, orange and white sweet potato, onions and Jerusalem artichokes. Season well with salt and pepper and toss gently so they are coated with the honey butter.

Trim the base of the garlic and wrap in foil. Add to the baking dish and place in the oven for 1 hour, turning the vegetables occasionally so they caramelise evenly. When cooked, remove the foil from the garlic and pop the cloves from their skin. Add to the other vegetables and serve.

REALLY EASY! | **75** MINUTES | SERVES **2**

DIAMOND-CUT
ROAST SWEET POTATO
AND SLIVERED GARLIC

Peel the sweet potato and halve lengthways. Using a strong, sharp knife, make 1 cm (1/2 inch) deep cuts in a diamond pattern in the peeled surface, 1.5–2 cm (5/8– 3/4 inch) apart. Be careful not to cut all the way through. Place, cut-side-up, on a baking tray.

Preheat the oven to 190°C (375°F/Gas 5). **Combine** the orange juice with the olive oil in a small bowl and season well with salt and freshly ground black pepper. Drizzle all over the sweet potato.

Scatter rosemary sprigs on top and roast inthe oven.s

Scatter garlic over the sweet potato and bake for a further 20–30 minutes, or until tender.

1 small orange sweet potato (about 14 cm/ 5 1/2 inches long and 6 cm/2 1/2 inches thick)

juice of 1/2 an orange

1/2 tablespoon olive oil

salt and freshly ground black pepper.

4 rosemary sprigs

1 garlic clove, finely sliced

REALLY EASY!

50 MINUTES

SERVES **2**

VEGAN

BREAKFAST, SNACKS AND STANDBYS

It's common knowledge that missing out on breakfast is not a good idea. Your body needs fuelling before the rigours of the day and if you don't get a healthy breakfast there is a danger that you will be snacking all day as your body attempts to make up for lost ground.

If you feel like a nibble, don't be tempted by crisps or chocolate. See if you can find something healthier and more filling to keep your hunger at bay. Always keep some fresh fruit close at hand to munch after supper or if you are feeling peckish.

CRUNCHY NUT MUESLI

500 g (1 lb 2 oz) rolled oats

125 g (4^1/$_2$ oz) bran cereal

150 g (5^1/$_2$ oz/1 cup) pistachio nuts, shelled and roughly chopped

160 g (5^1/$_4$ oz/1 cup) macadamia nuts, roughly chopped

100 g (1 cup/3^1/$_3$ oz) pecan nuts, roughly chopped

125 g (4^1/$_2$ oz) dried apples, chopped

125 g (4^1/$_2$ oz) dried apricots, chopped

125 ml (4 fl oz/^{1}/$_2$ cup) maple syrup

1 teaspoon natural vanilla extract

Oats are a great source of protein, B vitamins, calcium and fibre. They are one of the few grains that do not have the bran and germ removed during processing.

Preheat the oven to 180°C (350°F/Gas 4). Place oats, bran, pistachios, macadamias, pecans, dried apples and dried apricots in a bowl and mix to combine.

Place maple syrup and vanilla in a small pan and cook over low heat for 3 minutes or until syrup becomes runny and easy to pour.

Pour maple syrup over oat mixture and toss lightly to coat. Divide mixture between two non-stick baking dishes. Bake for 20 minutes or until the muesli is lightly toasted, turning frequently. Allow mixture to cool before transferring to an airtight container.

REALLY EASY! — **45** MINUTES — MAKES **1 kg** (2lbs 4oz) — VEGAN

PUFFED CORN CEREAL

Preheat the oven to 180°C (350°F/Gas 4). Spread out the corn, millet, fruit and nut mix, bran, coconut and pepitas in a large roasting tin.

Pour the maple syrup over the puffed corn mixture and stir until the dry ingredients are well coated.

Stir in the bran cereal and fruit salad mix and bake for 15 minutes, or until golden, turning the cereal several times during cooking. Cool completely before storing in an airtight container.

REALLY EASY!

25 MINUTES

MAKES 1½ kg (3lbs 2 oz)

VEGAN

85 g (3 oz) puffed corn

85 g (3 oz) puffed millet

2 x 200 g (7 oz) packets dried fruit and nut mix

180 g (6 oz) unprocessed natural bran

60 g (2¼ oz) flaked coconut

¹/₃ cup (60 g/2¼ oz) pepitas

³/₄ cup (185 ml/6 fl oz) maple syrup

1 cup (70 g/2½ oz) processed bran cereal

2 x 200 g (7 oz) packets dried fruit salad mix, cut into small pieces

FRUIT SALAD IN VANILLA, GINGER AND LEMONGRASS SYRUP

250 g (9 oz) watermelon, cubed

130 g (4½ oz) honeydew melon, cubed

¼ small pineapple, chopped

½ mango, diced

125 g (4½ oz) strawberries, halved

2 small mint sprigs

Lemongrass syrup

60 ml (2 fl oz/¼ cup) lime juice

20 g (¾ oz) soft brown sugar

½ stem lemongrass, finely sliced

1 tablespoon grated fresh ginger

1 small vanilla bean, split

If you prefer your syrup without the lemongrass pieces but like the flavour, bruise the white part of the lemongrass with a rolling pin, place in the syrup, cook and remove along with the vanilla bean.

Place the fruit and mint in a bowl and mix gently.

To **make** the syrup, place the lime juice, sugar and 125 ml (4 fl oz/½ cup) water in a small saucepan and stir over low heat until the sugar dissolves, then add the lemongrass, ginger and vanilla bean. Bring to the boil, reduce the heat and simmer for 10 minutes, or until reduced and slightly thickened. Remove the vanilla bean (and lemongrass if you prefer), pour the syrup over the fruit and refrigerate until cold.

REALLY EASY!

35 MINUTES + CHILLING TIME

SERVES **2**

VEGAN

BANANA SMOOTHIE

This drink is delicious with any other fresh fruit or drained tinned fruit-berries. Fruit-flavoured yoghurt will add even more flavour to your smoothie and soy milk is a delicious, healthy (vegan) alternative.

Put the bananas in a blender or food processor. Add the yoghurt, honey, wheat germ, milk and nutmeg.

Process or blend until smooth. Taste before serving and add more honey if you like.

REALLY EASY! · 5 MINUTES · SERVES 2 · VEGAN

2 bananas

60 g (2 oz/^{1}/$_4$ cup) plain yoghurt

1 tablespoon honey

2 tablespoons wheat germ

500 ml (17 fl oz/2 cups) milk

ground nutmeg, to taste

BREAKFAST SHAKE

150 g (5¹/₂ oz) fruit
(mango, strawberries,
blueberries, banana,
passionfruit, peach)

250 ml (9 fl oz/1 cup) milk

2 teaspoons wheat germ

1 tablespoon honey

60 g (2¹/₄ oz/¹/₄ cup)
vanilla yoghurt

1 egg, optional

1 tablespoon malt powder

If you are running late this simple shake will deliver a punch to keep you going until lunch.

Put all the ingredients in a blender and blend for 30 seconds to 1 minute, or until well combined. Pour into chilled glasses and serve.

REALLY EASY! 10 MINUTES SERVES 2

POACHED EGGS
WITH GARLIC YOGHURT DRESSING AND SPINACH

Poached eggs with a difference! The ideal way to start your weekend. You can use an egg poacher or egg ring rather than a frying pan if you prefer.

To make the dressing, **mix** together the yoghurt, garlic and chives.

Wash the spinach and place it in a large saucepan with just the little water that is left clinging to the leaves. Cover the pan and cook over low heat for 3–4 minutes, or until the spinach has wilted. Add the butter. Season. Set aside and keep warm. Cook the tomatoes under a hot grill for 3–5 minutes.

Fill a frying pan three-quarters full with cold water and add the vinegar and some salt to stop the egg whites spreading. Bring to a gentle simmer. Gently break the eggs one by one into a small bowl, then carefully slide each one into the water. Reduce the heat so that the water barely moves. Cook for 1–2 minutes, or until the eggs are just set. Remove with an egg flip. Drain.

Toast the bread. Top each slice of toast with spinach, an egg and some dressing. Serve with tomato halves.

REALLY EASY! · 25 MINUTES · SERVES 2

Dressing

60 g (2 oz) sheep's milk yoghurt

$1/4$ small garlic clove, crushed

$1/2$ tablespoon snipped fresh chives

150 g ($5^1/2$ oz) baby English spinach leaves

15 g ($1/2$ oz) butter, chopped

2 tomatoes, halved

$1/2$ tablespoon white vinegar

4 eggs

$1/2$ round loaf light rye bread, cut into 4 thick slices

BEAN NACHOS

2 large ripe tomatoes

1 ripe avocado, mashed

1/2 tablespoon lime juice

1/2 tablespoon sweet chilli sauce

1/2 tablespoon oil

1 small red onion, diced

1/2 small red chilli, chopped

1 teaspoon ground oregano

1 teaspoon ground cumin

pinch chilli powder

1/2 tablespoon tomato paste

125 ml (4 fl oz, 1/2 cup)
white wine

1 x 440 g (14 oz) can red kidney
beans, rinsed and drained

1 1/2 tablespoons chopped fresh
coriander leaves

100 g (3 1/4 oz) packet corn chips

45 g (1 1/2 oz) grated
cheddar cheese

sour cream, to serve

Score a cross in the base of each tomato. Put them in a bowl of boiling water for 30 seconds, then plunge into cold water and peel the skin away from the cross. Cut in half and scoop out the seeds with a teaspoon. Chop the tomato flesh.

Mix together the avocado, lime juice and sweet chilli sauce.

Heat the oil in a large frying pan. Cook the onion, chilli, oregano, cumin and chilli powder over medium heat for 2 minutes. Add the tomato, tomato paste and wine and cook for 5 minutes, or until the liquid reduces. Add the beans and coriander.

Divide the corn chips into two portions on heatproof plates. Top with the bean mixture and sprinkle with cheese. Flash under a hot grill until the cheese melts. Serve with the avocado mixture and sour cream.

REALLY EASY! · 30 MINUTES · SERVES 2

FRIED TOMATOES
WITH MARINATED HALOUMI

Haloumi is a firm, stretched-curd cheese that is matured in brine (salt water) . It has a salty, sharp taste similar to feta. I also like to serve haloumi as part of a cheese platter, together with fresh fruit. It can also be pan-fried in olive oil or brushed with oil before grilling. I love its smooth and creamy texture when it melts.

Place the haloumi and tomatoes in a non-metallic dish. Whisk together the garlic, lemon juice, balsamic vinegar, thyme and extra virgin olive oil in a jug and pour over the haloumi and tomatoes. Cover and marinate for 3 hours or overnight. Drain well, reserving the marinade.

Heat the olive oil in a large frying pan. Add the haloumi and cook in batches over medium heat for 1 minute each side, or until golden brown. Transfer to a plate and keep warm. Add the tomatoes and cook over medium heat for 5 minutes, or until their skins begin to burst. Transfer to a plate and keep warm.

Toast the bread until it is golden brown. Serve the fried haloumi on top of the toasted bread, piled high with the tomatoes and drizzled with the reserved marinade. Best served immediately.

200 g (7 oz) haloumi cheese, cut into eight 1 cm ($1/2$ inch) slices

125 g ($4 1/2$ oz) cherry tomatoes, halved

125 g ($4 1/2$ oz) teardrop tomatoes, halved

1 garlic clove, crushed

1 tablespoon lemon juice

$1/2$ tablespoon balsamic vinegar

1 teaspoon fresh lemon thyme

30 ml (1 fl oz) extra virgin olive oil

1 tablespoon olive oil

$1/2$ small loaf wholegrain bread, cut into 4 thick slices

EASY!

25 MINUTES + MARINATING TIME

SERVES 2

WARM ASPARAGUS
AND EGG SALAD WITH HOLLANDAISE

Hollandaise sauce

85 g (3 oz) butter

2 egg yolks

1/2 tablespoon lemon juice

2 eggs, at room temperature

160 g (5 oz) asparagus spears, trimmed

parmesan cheese shavings, to serve

To **make** the hollandaise, melt the butter in a small saucepan and skim off any froth. Remove from the heat and cool. Mix the egg yolks and tablespoons water in another small saucepan for 30 seconds, or until pale and foamy. Place the saucepan over very low heat and whisk for 2–3 minutes, or until thick and foamy—do not overheat or it will scramble. Remove from the heat. Gradually add the butter, whisking well after each addition (avoid using the whey at the bottom). Stir in the lemon juice and season. If the sauce is runny, return to the heat and whisk until thick—do not scramble.

Place the eggs in a saucepan half filled with water. Bring to the boil and cook for 6–7 minutes, stirring occasionally to centre the yolks. Drain and cover with cold water until cooled a little, then peel off the shells.

Plunge the asparagus into a large saucepan of boiling water and cook for 3 minutes, or until just tender. Drain and pat dry. Divide between two plates. Spoon on the hollandaise. Cut the eggs in half and arrange two halves on each plate. Sprinkle with parmesan shavings to serve.

EASY! · 20 MINUTES · SERVES 2

SCRAMBLED EGGS

I sometimes stir cheese, such such as gruyère, into my scrambled eggs for a delicious change. A healthier option is to stir through a handful of chopped fresh herbs. You can also add roasted vegetables such as pepper, tomato, onion and a few basil leaves to make Piperade.

Crack the eggs into a bowl, add the milk or cream and season well. Whisk gently with a fork until well combined.

Melt half the butter in a small pan or frying pan over low heat. Add the eggs, and stir constantly with a wooden spoon. Do not turn up the heat—scrambling must be done slowly and gently. When most of the egg has set, add the remaining butter and remove the pan from the heat. There should be enough heat left in the pan to finish cooking the eggs and melt the butter. Scrambled eggs should be creamy, not dry or rubbery. Serve immediately on toast—they will not sit even for a minute.

6 eggs

1 tablespoon milk or cream

50 g (1¾ oz) butter

2 slices toast

REALLY EASY! | 10 MINUTES | SERVES 2

Note: It is very important to use fresh eggs when scrambling. To check whether an egg is fresh put it in a bowl of cold water. If it sinks on its side it is fresh, and if it floats on its end it is stale. If it is somewhere between the two it is not perfectly fresh but still good enough to scramble.

LIGHT AND FLUFFY OMELETTES

3 eggs

10 g (¹/₄ oz) butter

¹/₂ teaspoon oil

Omelettes really aren't that difficult to make well but if you are making them for more than one person make each one separately. For the best results, use very fresh eggs. As a tasty variation add 30 g (1 oz) grated strong-tasting cheese, such as gruyère. Incidentally, three eggs may seem excessive for one person but it's well worth the extra expense.

Crack the eggs into a small bowl and add a teaspoon of water. Break them up with a fork but do not overbeat them—the yolks and whites should be just combined. Season well.

Melt the butter and oil in a non-stick or well-seasoned frying pan (15 cm/6 inches diameter is about the right size for 3 eggs). When the butter has melted, swirl it around the pan, turn up the heat and pour in the egg.

Tilt the pan to cover the base with egg and leave it for a few seconds. Using a spatula or egg flip, draw the sides of the omelette into the centre and let any extra liquid egg run to the outside. As soon as the egg is almost set, tip the pan on a 45-degree angle and flip one half of the omelette into the middle and then over again so you have a flat roll. Slide the omelette onto a plate and eat immediately. The egg will continue cooking inside the omelette.

REALLY EASY! 10 MINUTES SERVES 1

INDIVIDUAL OVEN-BAKED ROSTI

Preheat the oven to 220°C (425°F/Gas 7). Cook the potatoes in a pan of boiling salted water for 7 minutes, or until just tender. Drain.

Prepare a 6-hole muffin tin, with holes measuring 6 cm (2¹/₂ inches) at the top and 4.5 cm (1³/₄ inches) at the base, by brushing with a little of the butter. Grate the potatoes and onion, mix together in a bowl and pour the melted butter over the mixture. Season with salt and mix together well. Using two forks, divide the mixture among the muffin holes, gently pressing it in. Cook the rosti in the oven for 45 minutes, or until golden.

Using a small palette knife, **loosen** each rosti around the edge and lift out. Serve on a warm serving dish.

250 g (9 oz) waxy potatoes (desiree, pontiac), peeled

1 small onion

15 g (¹/₂ oz) butter, melted

EASY!

60 MINUTES

SERVES **2**

HASH BROWNS

400 g (13 oz) waxy
potatoes (desiree,
pontiac), peeled

---

60 g (2¼ oz) butter

These hash browns may take a little more effort than popping around the corner to the local fast food outlet does but it's time well spent as the results are delicious. Don't worry if you don't have egg rings, just cook as one large cake.

Boil or steam the potatoes until just tender. Drain, cool, chop coarsely and season with salt and pepper.

Heat half the butter in a large heavy-based frying pan and put four lightly greased egg rings into the pan. Spoon the potato evenly into the egg rings, filling the rings to the top and pressing the potato down lightly to form flat cakes. Cook over medium-low heat for 5–7 minutes, or until a crust forms on the bottom. Be careful not to burn. Shake the pan gently to prevent sticking.

Turn the hash browns with a large spatula. Gently loosen the egg rings and remove with tongs. Cook for another 4–5 minutes, or until browned and crisp. Remove from the pan and drain on paper towels. Add a little more butter to the pan, if necessary, and cook the remaining potato in the same way. Serve immediately.

REALLY EASY! · 30 MINUTES · SERVES 2

BRUSCHETTA

Each topping makes enough for four slices of bruschetta so you will only need four slices of bread if you only want to make one topping.

To make the classic Tuscan topping, **score** a cross in the base of each tomato and place in a bowl of boiling water for 10 seconds, then plunge into cold water. Peel the skin away from the cross. Cut in half and scoop out the seeds with a teaspoon. Finely dice the flesh, then combine with the basil, garlic and oil.

To make the mushroom and parsley topping, **heat** the oil in a frying pan and cook the mushrooms over medium heat for 5 minutes, or until just tender. Remove from the heat and transfer to a small bowl. Stir in the lemon juice, goat's cheese, parsley and thyme.

Toast the bread and, while still hot, rub with the cut side of a garlic clove. Drizzle oil over each slice of bread, then season with salt and freshly ground black pepper. Divide the toppings among the bread slices.

Classic Tuscan

3 ripe roma (plum) tomatoes

2 tablespoons basil, shredded

1 garlic clove, finely chopped

1 tablespoon extra virgin olive oil

Mushroom and parsley

1 tablespoon olive oil

100 g (3 1/2 oz) small button mushrooms, quartered

1/2 tablespoon lemon juice

25 g (1 oz) goat's cheese, crumbled

1/2 tablespoon finely chopped flat-leaf (Italian) parsley

1/2 teaspoon chopped thyme

8 slices crusty white Italian-style bread, cut into 1 cm (1/2 inch) slices

2 garlic cloves, halved

30 ml (1 fl oz) olive oil

CHARGRILLED ASPARAGUS WITH SALSA

2 eggs

1 tablespoon milk

1/2 tablespoon olive oil

1 corn cob

1/2 small red onion, diced

1/2 red pepper (capsicum), finely chopped

1 tablespoon chopped thyme

1 tablespoon olive oil, extra

1 tablespoon balsamic vinegar

12 fresh asparagus spears

1/2 tablespoon macadamia oil

toasted wholegrain bread, to serve

Beat the eggs and milk to combine. Heat the oil in a non-stick frying pan over medium heat, add the egg and cook until just set. Flip and cook the other side. Remove and allow to cool, then roll up and cut into thin slices.

Cook the corn in a chargrill pan (griddle) or in boiling water until tender. Allow to cool slightly, then slice off the corn kernels. Make the salsa by gently combining the corn, onion, pepper, thyme, extra olive oil and balsamic vinegar.

Trim off any woody ends from the asparagus spears, lightly brush with macadamia oil and cook in a chargrill pan (griddle) or on a barbecue hotplate until tender.

Serve the asparagus topped with a little salsa and the finely shredded egg, accompanied by fingers of buttered, toasted wholegrain bread.

REALLY EASY!   30 MINUTES   SERVES 2

ROASTED FIELD MUSHROOMS WITH TARRAGON AND LEMON CRÈME FRAÎCHE

Preheat the oven to 200°C (400°F/ Gas 6). In a large roasting tin, combine the oil, lemon juice and garlic. Add the mushrooms, and gently toss until coated. Season well with salt and pepper and arrange in a single layer. Roast for 30 minutes, turning to cook evenly.

Meanwhile, in a small bowl, **combine** the crème fraîche, lemon juice, garlic and tarragon.

Sprinkle the mushrooms and their cooking juices with parsley, and serve with the lemon crème fraîche and toasted bread.

REALLY EASY! · 45 MINUTES · SERVES 2

40 ml (1¼ fl oz) olive oil

1 tablespoon lemon juice

2 garlic cloves, crushed

6 large flat field mushrooms, brushed and stems trimmed

1 tablespoon finely chopped flat-leaf (Italian) parsley

toasted bread, to serve

Lemon crème fraîche

30 ml (1 fl oz) crème fraîche

1 teaspoon lemon juice

1 garlic clove, crushed

1 teaspoon chopped tarragon

PEPPERS ROLLED WITH GOAT'S CHEESE, BASIL AND CAPERS

2 large red capsicums (peppers)

1 tablespoon flat-leaf (Italian) parsley, chopped

1 tablespoon chives, snipped

1 tablespoon baby capers, finely chopped

1/2 tablespoon balsamic vinegar

75 g (2³/₄ oz) goat's cheese

8 basil leaves

olive oil, to cover

crusty Italian bread, to serve

I love the exquisitely rich and fragrant flavours that the balsamic vinegar adds to this dish.

Cut the pepper into large flat pieces and remove any seeds. Place on a tray skin-side up under a hot grill (broiler) until the skin blisters and blackens. Place in a plastic bag and leave to cool, then peel away the skin. Cut into 3 cm (1¹/₄ inch) wide pieces.

Combine the parsley, chives, capers and balsamic vinegar in a small bowl. Crumble in the goat's cheese, and mix well. Season with lots of pepper. Place a basil leaf on the inside of each capsicum piece, and top with a teaspoon of the goat's cheese mixture. Roll the capsicum over the goat's cheese and secure with a toothpick. Place in an airtight, non-reactive container and cover with olive oil. Refrigerate until required. Allow to return to room temperature before serving with crusty Italian bread.

REALLY EASY! 25 MINUTES SERVES 2

FRESH RICE PAPER ROLLS

To make the dipping sauce, **mix** together the chilli sauce and lime juice.

Place the vermicelli in a bowl, cover with boiling water and leave for 5 minutes, or until softened. Drain, then cut into short lengths.

Put the vermicelli, mango, cucumber, avocado, spring onion, coriander, mint, sweet chilli sauce and lime juice in a bowl and mix together well.

Working with no more than two rice paper wrappers at a time, **dip** each wrapper in a bowl of warm water for 10 seconds to soften, then lay out on a flat work surface. Put 1 tablespoon of the filling on the wrapper, fold in the sides and roll up tightly. Repeat with the remaining filling and rice paper wrappers. Serve immediately with the dipping sauce.

REALLY EASY! · 25 MINUTES · SERVES 2 (MAKES 10) · VEGAN

Note: Ensure the rice paper rolls are tightly rolled together or they will fall apart while you are eating them.

These rolls can be made 2–3 hours ahead of time — layer the rolls in an airtight container between sheets of greaseproof paper or plastic wrap, then store in the refrigerator.

Dipping sauce

30 ml (1 fl oz) sweet chilli sauce

1/2 tablespoon lime juice

50 g (1³/₄ oz) dried rice vermicelli

1/4 green mango, thinly sliced

1/2 small Lebanese (short) cucumber, seeded and thinly sliced

1/4 avocado, thinly sliced

2 spring onions (scallions), thinly sliced

2 tablespoons coriander (cilantro) leaves

1 tablespoon chopped Vietnamese mint

1/2 tablespoon sweet chilli sauce

1 tablespoon lime juice

10 square (15 cm/6 inch) rice paper wrappers

RED PEPPER AND WALNUT
DIP WITH TOASTED PITTA WEDGES

2 large red peppers (capsicums)

1/2 small red chilli

2 garlic cloves, in the skin

50 g (1 3/4 oz/1 cup) walnuts, lightly toasted

25 g (1 oz) sourdough bread, crusts removed

1 tablespoon lemon juice

1/2 tablespoon pomegranate molasses

1/2 teaspoon ground cumin

pitta bread

olive oil

sea salt

I always serve this dish with pitta wedges.

Cut the peppers into large flat pieces. Place on a tray skin-side up with the chilli and the whole garlic cloves, and cook under a hot grill (broiler) until the skin blackens and blisters. Transfer to a plastic bag and allow to cool. Gently peel away the capsicum and chilli skin, and remove the garlic skins.

Place the walnuts in a food processor and grind. Add the pepper and chilli flesh, garlic, bread, lemon juice, pomegranate molasses and cumin, and blend until smooth. Stir in 2 tablespoons of warm water to even out the texture, and season well with salt. Cover and refrigerate overnight so the flavours develop.

Preheat the oven to 200°C (400°F/ Gas 6). Cut the pitta bread into wedges, brush with olive oil and lightly sprinkle with sea salt. Cook in the oven for about 5 minutes, or until golden brown. Allow to cool and become crisp.

Drizzle olive oil over the dip. Serve with the toasted pitta wedges.

REALLY EASY! · 35 MINUTES + MARINATING TIME · SERVES 2 · VEGAN

ROAST PUMPKIN, FETA AND
PINE NUT PASTIE

Preheat the oven to 220°C (425°F/ Gas 7). Place the pumpkin on a baking tray and toss with the olive oil, garlic and salt and pepper. Roast in the oven for 40 minutes, or until cooked and golden. Remove and allow to cool.

Evenly **divide** the pumpkin among the four pastry squares, placing it in the centre. Top with the feta, oregano and pine nuts. Drizzle with a little of the feta marinating oil. Bring two of the diagonally opposite corners together and pinch in the centre above the filling. Bring the other two diagonally opposite corners together, and pinch to seal along the edges. The base will be square, the top will form a pyramid. Twist the top to seal where all four corners meet.

Place the egg yolk and milk in a small bowl, and whisk with a fork to make an eggwash for the pastry.

Place the pasties on a greased baking tray and brush with the eggwash. Sprinkle with sesame seeds and sea salt and bake for 15 minutes, or until golden brown.

EASY!

1 1/4 HOURS

SERVES 2

400 g (14 oz) Jap pumpkin, skin removed and cut into 1 cm (1/2 inch) thick slices

1 tablespoon olive oil

1 garlic clove, crushed

2 sheets butter puff pastry, cut into 15 cm (6 inch) squares

50 g (1 3/4 oz) marinated feta cheese

1 1/2 tablespoons oregano leaves, roughly chopped

1 tablespoon pine nuts, toasted

1/2 egg yolk

1/2 tablespoon milk

1/2 tablespoon sesame seeds

sea salt, to sprinkle

VEGETABLE DUMPLINGS

1/2 tablespoon oil

2 spring onions (scallions), sliced

1 garlic clove, chopped

1 teaspoon grated fresh ginger

2 tablespoons snipped garlic chives

210 g (7 1/2 oz) choy sum, (Chinese flower shredded

1 tablespoon sweet chilli sauce

1 1/2 tablespoons chopped coriander (cilantro) leaves

25 g (1 oz) water chestnuts, drained and chopped

15 gow gee wrappers

Dipping Sauce

1/4 teaspoon sesame oil

1/4 teaspoon peanut oil

1/2 tablespoon soy sauce

1/2 tablespoon lime juice

1/2 small red chilli, finely chopped

Heat the oil in a frying pan over medium heat and cook the spring onion, garlic, ginger and chives for 1–2 minutes, or until soft. Increase the heat to high, add the choy sum and cook for 4–5 minutes, or until wilted. Stir in the chilli sauce, coriander and water chestnuts. Allow to cool. If the mixture is too wet, squeeze dry.

Lay a wrapper on the work surface. Place a heaped teaspoon of the filling in the centre. Moisten the edge of the wrapper with water and pinch to seal, forming a ball. Trim. Repeat with the remaining wrappers and filling.

Half fill a wok with water and bring to the boil. Line a bamboo steamer with baking paper. Steam the dumplings, seam-side up, for 5–6 minutes.

To **make** the dipping sauce, combine all the ingredients. Serve with the dumplings.

EASY! | 35 MINUTES | MAKES 15 | VEGAN

STUFFED MUSHROOMS

Preheat the oven to 200°C (400°F/ Gas 6). Remove the stems from the mushrooms and discard. Wipe over the caps with a clean, damp cloth to remove any dirt.

Melt the butter in a small frying pan over medium heat, add the spring onion and cook for 2 minutes, or until soft. Add the crushed garlic and cook for another minute. Place the breadcrumbs in a bowl and pour in the spring onion mixture, then add the herbs, parmesan and beaten egg. Season with salt and freshly cracked black pepper and mix together well.

Lightly grease a baking tray. Divide the stuffing evenly among the mushrooms, pressing down lightly. Arrange the mushrooms on the tray, drizzle with olive oil and bake in the oven for 15 minutes, or until the tops are golden and the mushrooms are cooked through and tender. Serve immediately.

REALLY EASY! **30** MINUTES **SERVES 2**

4 large cap mushrooms

20 g ($^3/_4$ oz) butter

3 spring onions (scallions), chopped

$1^1/_2$ garlic cloves, crushed

100 g ($3^1/_2$ oz/1 cup) day-old breadcrumbs

$^3/_4$ tablespoon finely chopped oregano

1 tablespoon chopped flat-leaf (Italian) parsley

25 g (1 oz/$^1/_4$ cup) grated parmesan cheese

$^1/_2$ egg, lightly beaten

olive oil, for greasing and drizzling

BAKED STUFFED PEPPERS

1 red pepper (capsicum)

1 yellow pepper (capsicum)

1 teaspoon olive oil

8 basil leaves

1¼ tablespoons capers in vinegar, drained, rinsed and chopped

1½ tablespoons olive oil, extra

1 garlic clove, crushed

1½ teaspoons aged balsamic vinegar

Peppers are fruits not vegetables and can be stored in a plastic bag in the fridge for up to five days. Select those which are firm, with glossy, unwrinkled skin. Avoid dull-looking peppers with soft spots or blemishes.

Preheat the oven to 180°C (350°F/ Gas 4). Cut the pepper in half lengthways, leaving the stem intact (or if they are very large, cut them into quarters). Scrape out the seeds and any excess pith. Drizzle the bottom of an ovenproof dish with the oil, and add the peppers, skin-side down.

In each half pepper, **place** 2 basil leaves, then divide the chopped capers among them. Season well with salt and freshly ground pepper.

In a bowl, **combine** the extra oil with the garlic and balsamic vinegar, and drizzle evenly over the peppers. Cover the dish with foil, and cook for 10–15 minutes, or until the peppers have partially cooked.

Remove the foil, and cook for another 15–20 minutes, or until the peppers are tender and golden on the edges. Serve warm or at room temperature.

REALLY EASY! · 40 MINUTES · SERVES 2 · VEGAN

POTATO TORTILLA

Place the potato slices in a large saucepan, cover with cold water and bring to the boil over high heat. Boil for 5 minutes, then drain and set aside.

Heat the oil in a deep-sided non-stick frying pan over medium heat. Add the onion and garlic and cook for 5 minutes, or until the onion softens.

Add the potato and parsley to the pan and stir to combine. Cook over medium heat for 5 mintues, gently pressing down into the pan.

Whisk the eggs with 1 teaspoon each of salt and freshly ground pepper and pour evenly over the potato. Cover and cook over low–medium heat for about 20 minutes, or until the egg is just set. Slide onto a serving plate or serve directly from the pan.

250 g (9 oz) potatoes, cut into 1 cm ($^1/_2$ inch) slices

30 ml (1 oz) olive oil

$^1/_2$ brown onion, thinly sliced

2 garlic cloves, thinly sliced

1 tablespoon finely chopped flat-leaf (Italian) parsley

3 eggs

REALLY EASY! 45 MINUTES SERVES 2

UDON NOODLE SUSHI ROLLS

150 g (5½ oz) flat udon or soba noodles

3 sheets roasted nori

25 g (1 oz) pickled daikon, cut into long, thin strips

1½ tablespoons drained red pickled ginger shreds

ponzu sauce, for dipping

The ponzu sauce is of course optional but it does add a distinct flavour to this dish. The source is made from rice vinegar, soy, mirin and dashi and is widely available from Asian supermarkets.

Cook the udon or soba noodles according to the packet instructions or until tender. Rinse under cold water and pat dry.

Working on a flat surface, **lie** one sheet of nori on a sushi mat. Top with one-sixth of the noodles along the bottom half of the nori, then arrange the daikon and the pickled ginger along the centre of the noodles. Roll the nori up firmly to enclose the filling. Cut the roll in half and then each half into three equal pieces. Repeat with the remaining ingredients. Serve with the ponzu sauce.

REALLY EASY!

20 MINUTES

SERVES **2** (MAKES 18)

VEGAN

MUSHROOM PÂTÉ WITH MELBA TOAST

Heat the butter in a large frying pan. Cook the onion and garlic over medium heat for 2 minutes, or until soft. Increase the heat, add the mushrooms and cook for 5 minutes, or until the mushrooms are soft and most of the liquid has evaporated. Leave to cool for 10 minutes.

Place the almonds in a food processor or blender and chop roughly. Add the mushroom mixture and process until smooth. With the motor running, gradually pour in the cream. Stir in the herbs and season with salt and cracked black pepper. Spoon into two 250 ml (9 fl oz/1 cup) ramekins and smooth the surface. Cover and refrigerate for 4–5 hours to allow the flavours to develop.

To make the toast, **preheat** the oven to 180°C (350°F/Gas 4). Toast one side of the bread under a hot grill (broiler) until golden. Remove the crusts and cut each slice into four triangles. Place on a large oven tray in a single layer, toasted-side down, and cook for 5–10 minutes, or until crisp. Remove as they crisp. Spread with pâté and serve immediately.

25 g (1 oz) butter

1/2 small onion, chopped

1 1/2 garlic cloves, crushed

185 g (6 1/2 oz) button mushrooms, quartered

60 g (2 1/4 oz/1/2 cup) slivered almonds, toasted

1 tablespoon cream

1 tablespoon finely chopped thyme

1 1/2 tablespoons finely chopped flat-leaf (Italian) parsley

3 thick slices wholegrain or wholemeal bread

REALLY EASY!

25 MINUTES + STANDING TIME

SERVES 2 (MAKES 12)

TEMPURA VEGETABLES
WITH WASABI MAYONNAISE

Wasabi mayonnaise

1 tablespoon whole-egg mayonnaise

1 1/2 teaspoons wasabi paste

1/4 teaspoon grated lime zest

1 egg yolk

125 ml (4 fl oz/1/2 cup) chilled soda water

15 g (1/2 oz) cornflour (cornstarch)

55 g (2 oz) plain (all-purpose) flour

20 g (3/4 oz) sesame seeds, toasted

oil, for deep-frying

1/2 small aubergine (eggplant), cut into thin rounds

1 small onion, cut into thin rounds, with rings intact

150 g (5 1/2 oz) orange sweet potato, cut into thin rounds

To make the wasabi mayonnaise, **combine** all the ingredients. Transfer to a serving bowl, cover with plastic wrap and refrigerate.

Place the egg yolks and soda water in a jug and mix lightly with a whisk. Sift the cornflour and flour into a bowl. Add the sesame seeds and a good sprinkling of salt and mix well. Pour the soda water and egg yolk mixture into the flour and stir lightly with a fork or chopsticks until just combined but still lumpy.

Fill a deep heavy-based saucepan or wok one-third full of oil and heat until a cube of bread dropped into the oil browns in 15 seconds. Dip pairs of the vegetables — aubergine and onion or aubergine and sweet potato — into the batter and cook in batches for 3–4 minutes, or until golden brown and cooked through. Drain on crumpled paper towels; season well. Keep warm, but do not cover or the tempura coating will go soggy.

Transfer the tempura to a warmed serving platter and serve immediately with the wasabi mayonnaise.

EASY! **35** MINUTES SERVES **2**

ORANGE SWEET POTATO WEDGES
WITH TANGY CUMIN MAYONNAISE

The tangy cumin mayonnaise really sets this dish apart from all others.

Preheat the oven to 200°C (400°F/ Gas 6). Place the olive oil in a large roasting tin and heat in the oven for 5 minutes.

Place the sweet potato in the tin in a single layer, season with salt and pepper and bake for 35 minutes, turning occasionally.

While the sweet potato is cooking, **place** the mayonnaise, lime juice, honey, coriander and cumin in a food processor, and blend until smooth.

Drain the wedges on crumpled paper towels and serve with the tangy cumin mayonnaise on the side.

REALLY EASY!

55 MINUTES

SERVES 2

1 1/4 tablespoons olive oil

500g (1 lb 2 oz) orange sweet potato, peeled and cut into 6 cm (2 1/2 inch) long wedges

100 g (3 1/2 oz) mayonnaise

30 ml (1 fl oz) lime juice

1/2 teaspoon honey

1/2 heaped tablespoon roughly chopped coriander (cilantro)

3/4 teaspoon ground cumin

BEETROOT HUMMUS

250 g (9 oz) beetroot

40 ml (1¼ oz) olive oil

1 small onion, chopped

½ tablespoon ground cumin

200 g (7 oz) tin chickpeas, drained

½ tablespoon tahini

40 g (1½ oz) plain yoghurt

1½ garlic cloves, crushed

30 ml (1 oz) lemon juice

60 ml (2 fl oz/¼ cup) vegetable stock

Lebanese or Turkish bread, to serve

I love beetroot but you can use 250 g (9 oz) of any vegetable to make the hummus. Try carrot or pumpkin.

Scrub the beetroot well. Bring a large saucepan of water to the boil over high heat and cook the beetroot for 35–40 minutes, or until soft and cooked through. Drain and cool slightly before peeling.

Meanwhile, **heat** 1 tablespoon of the oil in a frying pan over medium heat and cook the onion for 2–3 minutes, or until soft. Add the cumin and cook for a further 1 minute, or until fragrant.

Chop the beetroot and place in a food processor or blender with the onion mixture, chickpeas, tahini, yoghurt, garlic, lemon juice and stock, and process until smooth. With the motor running, add the remaining oil in a thin steady stream. Process until the mixture is thoroughly combined. Serve the hummus with Lebanese or Turkish bread.

REALLY EASY! — 50 MINUTES — SERVES 2 — VEGAN

TEX MEX CHILLI BEANS

It is said that red kidney beans originated in Mexico approximately 5000 years ago. Red kidney beans contain dietary fibre, iron, potassium, and several B vitamins. Tinned chickpeas, drained and rinsed, may be substituted for kidney beans in this recipe if you prefer.

Heat the oil, garlic, chillies and onion in a heavy-based pan and cook over medium heat for 3 minutes or until onion is golden.

Add the green pepper, kidney beans, undrained, chopped tomatoes, salsa and sugar. Bring to the boil, reduce heat and simmer, uncovered, for 15 minutes or until the sauce thickens. Chilli Beans can be served with sour cream, guacamole and corn chips.

REALLY EASY! · **25 MINUTES** · **SERVES 2** · **VEGAN**

1/2 tablespoon oil

1 garlic clove, crushed

1 small fresh red chilli, finely chopped

1 small onion, finely chopped

1/2 green pepper (capsicum), chopped

220 g (7³/₄ oz) tinned red kidney beans, drained and rinsed

220 g (7³/₄ oz) tinned peeled tomatoes

60 g (2¹/₄ oz) ready-made tomato salsa

1/2 teaspoon soft brown sugar

SESAME TOFU BITES

These bites taste delicicious but you really do have to leave them to marinate for two full hours or else the flavour will be impaired. Use soy yoghurt for a vegan option

Rinse and cut firm tofu into 2.5 cm (1 inch) cubes. Place the tofu in a shallow dish with crushed garlic, ginger, soft brown sugar and salt-reduced soy sauce. Cover and refrigerate for about 2 hours and then drain well.

Combine sesame seeds, cornflour and wholemeal plain flour in a large mixing bowl. Add the tofu cubes and toss to coat in the sesame-flour mixture. Heat oil in a frying pan. Add the tofu in batches and cook until golden. Drain on paper towels.

To make a chilli dipping sauce, **place** sweet chilli sauce, lime juice, fresh coriander and yoghurt in a small bowl and stir well to combine.

REALLY EASY! | **35** MINUTES + MARINATING TIME | SERVES **2** | VEGAN

250 g (9 oz) firm tofu

1 garlic clove, crushed

1 tablespoon fresh ginger, grated

$1/2$ tablespoon soft brown sugar

40 ml ($1^{1/4}$ fl oz) salt-reduced soy sauce

75 g ($2^{1/2}$ oz) sesame seeds

$1/2$ tablespoon cornflour

1 tablespoon wholemeal plain (all purpose) flour

30 ml (1 fl oz) oil

Dipping Sauce

1 tablespoon sweet chilli sauce

1 tablespoon lime juice

1 tablespoon fresh coriander (cilantro), chopped

100 g ($3^{1/2}$ oz) thick natural yoghurt

DUKKAH WITH FLAT BREAD

3 small pitta breads

Dukkah

25 g (1 oz) white sesame seeds

1 tablespoon coriander seeds

1 tablespoon cumin seeds

25 g (1 oz) hazelnuts, chopped

¹/₂ teaspoon salt

¹/₄ teaspoon ground black pepper

extra virgin olive oil, to serve

This is a traditional spice and nut mix from North Africa. It makes a delicious dip served with bread and olive oil and is also good sprinkled over salads. Stored in an airtight container, the mix will last for several weeks.

Heat a frying pan and separately dry-fry the sesame, coriander and cumin seeds and the hazelnuts for 1–2 minutes, or until they brown and start to release their aroma. Allow to cool and then process in a food processor until roughly ground. Transfer to a bowl and season with the salt and pepper.

REALLY EASY! · **15** MINUTES · SERVES **2** · VEGAN

ROASTED AUBERGINE DIP

Preheat the oven to 220°C (425°F/Gas 7). Prick the aubergine several times with a fork and put on a baking tray. Bake for 40–50 minutes, or until the skin is wrinkled and the aubergine appears collapsed. Remove from the oven and set aside to cool.

Dry-fry the cumin in a frying pan over medium heat for 1–2 minutes, or until the colour deepens and the cumin gives off its fragrant aroma. Set aside to cool.

Cut open the aubergine, scoop the flesh into a sieve and drain for 5 minutes. Chop the aubergine flesh until finely diced. Put into a bowl and stir in the cumin, garlic, lemon juice, oil and coriander and season with salt and pepper to taste.

Grill (broil) the Lebanese bread, cut into fingers and serve with the dip.

$1/2$ large aubergine (eggplant)

1 teaspoon ground cumin

1 garlic clove, crushed

juice of $1/4$ lemon

1 tablespoon extra virgin olive oil

1 tablespoon chopped coriander (cilantro) leaves

Lebanese (large pitta) bread, to serve

REALLY EASY! **60 MINUTES** **SERVES 2** **VEGAN**

CAYENNE SPICED ALMONDS

3/4 teaspoons
cayenne pepper

1/2 teaspoon ground
cumin

1/4 teaspoon
smoked paprika

1/4 teaspoon caster
(superfine) sugar

1 teaspoons
sea salt flakes

1/2 tablespoon olive oil

125 g (41/2 oz/3/4 cup)
blanched almonds

Combine the cayenne, cumin, paprika, sugar and salt in a large bowl and set aside.

Put the oil and almonds in a saucepan over medium heat and stir for 10 minutes, or until golden. Remove with a slotted spoon, add to the spice mix and toss to combine.

Cool to room temperature, tossing occasionally and serve.

REALLY EASY! 15 MINUTES SERVES 2 VEGAN

TAMARI NUT MIX

This is an ideal recipe for those late-night study sessions or even and end-of-exam party. Pepitas are peeled pumpkin seeds—they are available at most supermarkets and health-food stores. If the mix becomes soft once you have stored it for a while, spread the mix flat on a baking tray and bake in a slow (150°C/300°F/Gas 2) oven for 5–10 minutes.

Preheat the oven to 140°C (275°F/Gas 1). Lightly grease two large baking trays.

Place the mixed nuts, pepitas, sunflower seeds, cashew nuts and macadamia nuts in a large bowl. Pour the tamari over the nuts and seeds and toss together well, coating them evenly in the tamari. Leave for 10 minutes.

Spread the nut and seed mixture evenly over the baking trays and bake for 20–25 minutes, or until dry roasted. Cool completely and store in an airtight container for up to 2 weeks.

250 g (9 oz) mixed nuts (almonds, brazil nuts, peanuts, walnuts)

125 g (4$\frac{1}{2}$ oz) pepitas

125 g (4$\frac{1}{2}$ oz) sunflower seeds

125 g (4$\frac{1}{2}$ oz) cashew nuts

125 g (4$\frac{1}{2}$ oz) macadamia nuts

125 ml (4 fl oz/$\frac{1}{2}$ cup) tamari

REALLY EASY! · 35 MINUTES · SERVES 10 · VEGAN

SALT AND PEPPER TOFU PUFFS

1 x 190 g (6^3/$_4$ oz) packet fried tofu puffs

125 g (4^1/$_2$ oz) cornflour

1 tablespoon salt

^{1}/$_2$ tablespoon ground white pepper

1 teaspoon caster (superfine) sugar

2 egg whites, lightly beaten

peanut oil, for deep-frying

60 ml (2 fl oz) sweet chilli sauce

3 tablespoons lemon juice

lemon wedges, to serve

It is best to use a good-quality peanut oil to deep-fry the tofu puffs—the flavour will be slightly nutty. Tofu puffs are avaialble at Asian supermarkets.

Cut the tofu puffs in half and pat dry with paper towels.

Mix the cornflour, salt, pepper and caster sugar in a large bowl.

Dip the tofu puffs into the egg white in batches, then toss in the cornflour mixture, shaking off any excess.

Fill a deep heavy-based saucepan or wok one-third full of oil and heat until a cube of bread dropped into the oil browns in 15 seconds. Cook the tofu puffs in batches for 1–2 minutes, or until crisp. Drain well on paper towels.

Place the sweet chilli sauce and lemon juice in a bowl and mix together well. Serve immediately with the tofu puffs and lemon wedges.

REALLY EASY! 25 MINUTES SERVES 2

CORN FRITTERS

Sift the flour, baking powder, coriander and cumin into a bowl; make a well in the centre. Add the corn kernels, creamed corn, milk, egg, chives, salt and pepper. Stir until combined.

Heat the oil in a large non-stick pan. Lower heaped tablespoonsful of the mixture into the pan about 2 cm (³/₄ inch) apart, flatten slightly. Cook over medium-high heat 2 minutes or until underside is golden. Turn over; cook other side. Remove and drain on paper towels; repeat with the remaining mixture. Serve with dipping sauce.

To make Dipping Sauce: Heat vinegar, sugar, sambal oelek, chives and soy in small pan for 1–2 minutes until sugar is dissolved.

REALLY EASY!   40 MINUTES   SERVES 2

75 g (2¹/₂ oz) plain (all purpose) flour

³/₄ teaspoon baking powder

¹/₄ teaspoon ground coriander

pinch ground cumin

65 g (2¹/₂ oz) tinned corn kernels, well-drained

115 g (4 oz) tinned creamed-style corn

60 ml (2 fl oz/¹/₄ cup) milk

1 egg, lightly beaten

1 tablespoon snipped fresh chives

salt and pepper

60 ml (2 fl oz) olive oil

Dipping Sauce

¹/₂ tablespoon brown vinegar

1¹/₂ teaspoons soft brown sugar

¹/₂ teaspoon sambal oelek or chilli sauce

¹/₂ tablespoon snipped fresh chives

¹/₄ teaspoon soy sauce

ONION BHAJIS WITH SPICY TOMATO SAUCE

Spicy Tomato Sauce

1 small red chilli, chopped

¼ red pepper (capsicum), diced

100 g (3½ oz) tin chopped tomatoes

1 garlic clove, finely chopped

½ tablespoon soft brown sugar

⅓ tablespoon cider vinegar

30 g (1 oz) plain (all purpose) flour

1 teaspoon baking powder

pinch chilli powder

pinch ground turmeric

½ teaspoon ground cumin

1 egg, beaten

2 large handfuls chopped fresh coriander (cilantro) leaves

2 onions, very thinly sliced

oil, for deep-frying

To make the sauce, **combine** all the ingredients with 1½ tablespoons water in a saucepan. Bring to the boil, then reduce the heat and simmer for 20 minutes, or until the mixture thickens. Remove from the heat.

To make the bhajis, **sift** the flour, baking powder, spices and ½ teaspoon salt into a bowl and make a well in the centre. Gradually add the combined egg and 1½ tablespoons water, whisking to make a smooth batter. Stir in the coriander and onion.

Fill a deep heavy-based saucepan one-third full of oil and heat until a cube of bread dropped into the oil browns in 15 seconds. Drop tablespoons of the mixture into the oil and cook in batches for 90 seconds each side, or until golden. Drain on paper towels. Serve with the spicy tomato sauce.

EASY! · 35 MINUTES · SERVES 2

GARLIC MUSHROOMS

Try and buy red onions for this recipe as they are milder than ordinary onions and have a sweet flavour.

Heat the oil in frying pan, add the onions and garlic cook very gently for 15 minutes until very soft and golden brown. Season well.
Toast the bread and spread with the mayonnaise. Pile on the onions, cover with the cheese and place under a preheated grill for 2–3 minutes until the cheese is bubbling. Eat immediately.

2 tablespoons olive oil

2 red onions,
thinly sliced

1 garlic clove,
thinly sliced

seasoning

1 thick slice
country bread

1 tablespoon
mayonnaise

60g (2 oz) mozzarella or
cheddar cheese,
thinly sliced

INDEX